What Will the Neighbors Say?

Patricia H. Berne
Louis M. Savary

WHAT WILL THE NEIGHBORS SAY?

Facing the Fear of Disapproval

CONTINUUM · NEW YORK

1982

The Continuum Publishing Company
575 Lexington Avenue
New York, N.Y. 10022

Printed in the United States of America

Library of Congress Cataloging in Publication Data

Berne, Patricia H.
What will the neighbors say?

Includes bibliographical references.
1. Conformity. 2. Persuasion (Psychology)
3. Social acceptance. I. Savary, Louis M.
II. Title.
BF637.P4B38 1982 158'.2 82-14076
ISBN 0-8264-0196-1

Contents

Acknowledgments

For suggesting avenues of theory and research, we thank M. Patricia Golden, Jack Levin, Mary Quigley, Harriet R. Swankin, and Richard Woodward. For compiling a bibliography of supplementary books, we thank Olga Neft and Bruce Abbott. For providing questionnaire respondents, we thank Pamela Stewart, Theresa Suruda, Jack Levin, and graduate students in our classes at Sacred Heart University. For editorial comments and painstakingly accurate typing, we thank Helen P. Rauch. Finally, we thank the many people, kept anonymous in these pages, who shared personal stories about fear of what the neighbors might say.

PART ONE

Understanding the Fear

CHAPTER 1

Who We Are

Sticks and stones may break my bones,
But names will never hurt me!

Although for ages children have been using this taunt to defend themselves against the negative comments of other children, its claim is false. Name-calling is destructive. Malicious labeling does hurt people, and perhaps has created deeper and more long-lasting personality damage than all the sticks and stones that were ever wielded. Among children, however, there is a saving grace in their name-calling, for it is usually frank and open, and thus able to be denied or at least confronted.

Fear of Neighbors

Among adults, when the comment "What will the neighbors say?" is made or felt, it often triggers fear of disapproval and other strong emotional responses. For example, some people are so strongly influenced in their decisions by fear of what neighbors might say that they act as if neighbors really do have the right to tell them what choices to make and how to live their lives.

This old cliché, which became the title of our book, has power because of its familiarity and because of the inner fears it can sometimes trigger in us. "What can the neighbors be saying?" we wonder. "What judgments can they be making about me?" As we will suggest, people's inner fears are frequently activated when they wonder about neighbors' comments. For example, if I fear being labeled incompetent or unfriendly, it may be because there are some questions and doubts inside me about my competency and friendliness. Naturally, once my inner fear is activated, I also begin to suspect people outside can see through my mask of competency and friendliness. Then I begin wondering what people are thinking about me and fearing what they might say.

Who are the *neighbors* we talk about in this book? They include everyone who might react to me and evaluate me or label me. According to the results of our questionnaire, presented in Part Two, important neighbors include not only the people who live next door, but also family, relatives, friends, as well as people at work, school, church, and so on.

Why am I afraid of what they say? My fear is that their reaction to me might lead them to say unkind things about me, and that their comments would influence my self-image and their image of me. I want them to approve me, like me, and accept me. If they don't, I'm not sure what might happen to me.

Fear of disapproval is a very powerful reinforcer of socially approved behavior. We all fear being labeled in ways that would stir up this fear. Because there is a deep desire in all of us for social approval, the threat of its withdrawal by significant others is critical. According to researcher Collette Dowling, fear of disapproval seems to affect women more than men. In her book *The Cinderella Complex,* she reports how in our culture young girls, much more so than young boys, are trained to a lifetime role of passivity and dependency. This dependency is maintained and deepened in women by conditioning them to a need for continuous approval and a fear of disapproval. For example, while boys seem to enjoy the mastery of skills for the sake of mastery and eventual independence from adults, girls are more likely to achieve mastery not for its own sake but *for the sake of approval.* In other words, girls are customarily taught to anticipate the expectation of their neighbors and conform to them, and to fear disapproval if they don't. Although both men and women fear disapproval, women, according to Dowling, seem more vulnerable to it.

A Book about You

Because each of us wants to be welcomed and belong, this book is about all of us: how we fear being misunderstood, how we fear not being liked and loved, how we fear not being seen as the person we want to be seen as, not only by the people we care about but also by the larger world. We have all known in ourselves the childlike desire to be liked by everybody. At times we can all feel the wish to be the center of the universe, wanting everything to be focused on us and wanting it all to be good. Again and again, however, this childhood wish's reverse side is experienced. We are focused on, but not approved and not liked. At times the comments of others leave us with a fear of being exposed, misunderstood, and misjudged. This fear can eat away at our self-confidence.

Fear of what the neighbors might say comes from two sources: the people outside me whose voices I hear and the neighbors whom I have internalized, whose voices I hear even when no one is around.

Therefore, on one level, this book is about you and your relationship to yourself, helping you to listen carefully to the voices within you. It will ask you questions such as: How do you view yourself? What are the things about yourself you try to hide from yourself? Do you sometimes act as your own critical neighbor? How do you relate to the voices, urgings, and judgments you sense inside you? How do you react to them? How important are they to you? Is there a small voice deep within you that you miss listening to at all?

On another level, this book is about your relationships to other people, and will help you to listen carefully to their voices. It will ask you questions such as: Whose voices do you listen to most carefully? Whose voices do you not bother to listen to closely? Do you tend to listen for negative comments? How important to you is what others say about you? Do you prefer to listen to your inner voices?

Your Own Truth

As you become aware of how the fear of the neighbors works, you will learn to deal not only with your fears, but with your hopes and wants. We hope to suggest some possible pathways in looking for that elusive thing in each of us that is our own truth. Thus, ultimately, this is a book about searching for truth, and how people can laugh and cry together as they search to grow toward their truth.

All through years of schooling, wise teachers told us we should search for truth, but nobody quite told us what truth was or how we would recognize it. Despite all the thinking of philosophers and the voluminous research of scientists, we still don't have a clear answer to the question "What is truth?" But we do know it has something to do with who we are. Truth seems to be more a lived choice than simply an intellectual concept. We hope that, in exploring fears of neighbors' comments, we will learn to see clearly what we hope to be and are called to be; and in discovering this personal truth about ourselves, we will find ways to let the neighbors' voices be helpful and supportive rather than harmful and destructive.

A Positive Side

We may begin the task of finding our personal truth by examining the words and labels spoken by others about ourselves. Although we don't like to be the object of name-calling, since it often implies being judged, criticized, and devalued, we do realize there can be a positive side to words and labels spoken about us, that is, people can name us in affirmative ways.

The early Christians had a process called "naming gifts."

These gifts—talents, skills, innate abilities, personality qualities, etc.—were presumed to come from the Holy Spirit, and they were given to individuals for the building up of their neighborhood communities. When the early Christians recognized a quality or potential in another, they would name that quality and call it forth to be recognized in the community. There, the neighborly voices were affirmative and supportive. Their naming gave value to individuals and assured them of belonging to the community.

The naming of gifts still continues in Christian churches. Some years ago, one of the people in a church choir told a young man's mother that he had a beautiful voice. This naming invited the mother to take the time to listen to her son's voice and realize his talent. Just to make sure, she took him to a voice teacher, who affirmed his potential. The young man eventually made his way to the Metropolitan Opera Company. He now shares his gift with thousands of people.

Many things neighbors say about us can be seen as positive and helpful. Our belief is that people can learn to listen to affirmations, instead of focusing exclusively on their fears of negative labels.

There is no doubt that people are influenced in some way by the comments made by their friends and family, even in everyday conversations. We want to help people become conscious of that influence and to use it effectively. Even when people say things that might be taken as disapproval, we often have a choice to treat such comments not as a wound to our self-esteem but as an insight for our development as a person. As one woman put it, "In conversation, I'm aware sometimes that something someone says catches my attention. I'm stopped in my tracks. I hear what they're saying on a different level than other things they've said. This new kind of hearing sometimes hurts, but it also rings bells and raises questions. And I'm challenged to respond. I'm challenged to let go of my distortions and fears, choose a positive perspective for hearing my voice, and make a choice about my life."

It takes courage to come to know ourselves: to acknowledge

who we are and who we are not, what we are capable of and what we are not. It takes even more courage to make choices about ourselves. We are now at a time in world history when it's becoming important to take responsibility, as individuals and as nations, for how we are known and what we are known for, for standing up for who we are and what we value. Values, goals, and visions are some of the things people need to sort out in order to be in touch with their own personal truth.

For most of us today, the actual fear of what the people next door might say about us is not really as strong as it was in earlier generations. Though our parents may have anxiously peeked out from behind curtains to see if their neighbors were looking and judging, we seem to be less bothered by fear of next-door neighbors' comments, and our children are even less so. What has not changed, however, is the sensitivity and curiosity people have about how they are perceived by others. We still want to become members of society, and we still want to fit in, to be accepted, to belong. There will always be neighbors, as long as we want to be liked and approved. And the underlying need to develop our self-image still remains. Developing our self-image is a process strongly influenced by the continual feedback we receive from others in our lives, verbally or nonverbally, especially during our formative years.

The creation of one's self-image is strongly influenced by others. In dealing with their comments, the challenge is to move from an attitude of fear of what neighbors say about us to an attitude of sensitivity and curiosity. To be sensitive and curious in this way has two effects. First, it makes us vulnerable to what others say about us, and thus teaches us to be open and to listen. Second, it makes us potentially able to use this information to help our growth as individuals and as relating persons. This sensitivity and curiosity touches our human spirit. Developing a healthy self-image and learning our own personal truth become a spiritual journey, once the response to others grows beyond the level of fearing disapproval or rejection. The wish to be self-actualized to our fullest potential is a spiritual quest.

Each of the social sciences has something important to say about neighbors and their comments. In the following four chapters, we will take a look at how concern over what the neighbors might say is treated, in turn, by sociologists, anthropologists, social psychologists, and psychologists.

CHAPTER 2

Gossiping Neighbors: A Sociological Perspective

When we talk about what the neighbors might say, according to many sociologists, we are naturally talking about gossip. For it is through the medium of gossip that much of what neighbors say gets said.

Gossip is not merely "idle chatter," which is its common definition, but *small talk with a social purpose.* Sociologist Ralph L. Rosnow calls gossip a valuable social commodity. Among its functions, he lists gossip's capacity to entertain, to inform, to manipulate, to comfort, and to conserve the status quo. Thus, although gossip may be entertaining and informative to the listener, it is often used by the neighbors as an instrument of socialization, that is, of getting people to do what society expects them to.

Setting Standards

Gossip is often malicious, but not always so. Research by Northeastern University sociologist Jack Levin and colleagues shows that people's gossip is more often positive and complimentary than negative and derogatory. Specifically, in studies of newspaper gossip columnists, they found that "gossip columns tended to stress public recognition of socially approved behavior, while generally ignoring the negative sanction." Studying statistically the occurrences of gossip about occupational activity and private lives, they found that fully 30 percent of all occupational gossip received explicit approval of the columnists, for example, how well a star performed in a new show, while only six percent expressed disapproval; and of gossip regarding private lives and personal behavior of personalities in the newspaper columns, 77 percent involved expressions of approval, not disapproval. When there was disapproval, it was usually about minor infractions of everyday rules, eccentricities rather then evils. Levin and Kimmel found examples of disapproval such as Martha Raye ostentatiously displaying her mink stole, Redd Foxx refusing to attend his daughter's wedding because his estranged wife excluded his name from the invitation, and Catherine Deneuve announcing she would pose nude for *Playboy* magazine.

What research does show is that the small talk of gossip has a strong *normative* basis. At least half of gossip, whether it's carried on by newspaper columnists or suburban families, is primarily concerned with the prescription of certain behaviors and the proscription of others.

James West, who studied the social dynamics of a small American town he called Plainville, found gossiping to be at the center of social life. The various groups that gossiped did so primarily to maintain standards in the town. Merchant groups, gambler groups, congregations, old men, old women, even the "wild set"—all were devoted to using gossip to enforce and maintain the traditional morality and values of their community.

"Gossip about the past is a way in which a group thrusts its roots back into the past, creating a past history for the members in relation to one another," wrote sociologist Alexander Rysman. Since gossiping is enjoyable and tends to take place between friends, it helps tie relationships together. In fact, says Rysman, "the more exclusive a group, the greater its gossiping." He says professional groups such as lawyers, social scientists, and other high-status groups that want to exclude others gossip a great deal with their professional neighbors, since exclusiveness increases motivation to preserve group unity and solidarity.

Sally Yerkovich, professor at the University of Pennsylvania and expert in the ethnography of speaking, has clarified three important differences between gossiping and the simple exchange of information about absent people. First, to be able to gossip together, individuals must *know one another*. Second, the gossiper's comments must have a *moral quality*, that is, they must not only describe an individual's behavior but also present it as inviting sanction and evaluations, whether good or bad. Thus, the content of the gossip is often not as important as the evaluative or "moral" interaction that the talking supports. Third, hearers of the gossip need to know enough about the target person to experience the *excitement of revelation*.

Children's Gossip

Gossip is not reserved to adults. Children gossip from the time they can talk and begin to recognize others. Developmental psychologist Elizabeth Nolan observed that three-year-olds tend to talk about the traits and actions of other children who are not present. Children soon learn they are talked about by others and begin to be concerned with what others might say about them.

If the gossip of very young children often occurs without evaluation and judgment, the gossip of four- and five-year-olds, reports sociologist Gary Alan Fine, sounds remarkable similar in form to the gossip of adults. Gossip seems to take a central place in conversations among young children, as it does among adolescents, among college students, and among adults.

Perhaps a closer look at children's gossip will show how strongly it affects the personality and development of individuals, even at a very early age.

Four Effects of Gossip

Gary Alan Fine lists four effects of children's gossip, which to us seem to apply to all age groups as powerful influences in the personal choices and behavior of gossipers, as well as those being gossiped about.

First, the transfer of information in gossiping has a *socializing effect*. Through gossip one learns how to be sexual, how to be aggressive, how to behave in groups, what to say, what not to say. For children, gossip is one way to learn about the facts of life. Gossip among more mature members of society allows those less mature to learn vicariously how to behave when their turn arrives.

Second, the transfer of information in gossiping often carries with it a *normative effect*. "Most gossip," writes Fine, "carries explicitly or implicitly some perspective on the behavior that is being described." Gossip allows judgments to be made, norms to be stated and reaffirmed. Another word for all this is conformity. Joyce Maynard, in her book *Looking Back*, described a fifth-grade girl's sensitivity to the normative function of peer gossip.

> We knew each other's faces and bodies and wardrobes so well that any change was noticed at once, the fuel for endless notes. That is why I dressed so carefully mornings—I was about to face the scrutiny of fifteen gossip-seeking girls, ten only slightly less observant boys ready to imitate my voice and walk. . . . At every moment—even at home with no one but family there—I'd be conscious of what the other kids, The Group, would think if they could see me now.

An interesting note about preadolescents and teens is that their damning judgments on peers seem to have much greater impact than similar judgments among adults. Moreover, malicious gossip among children is often swift and sure, since few links are needed before the comments get back to the target child. Public gossip, that is, where the object of the gossip is actually present among the gossiping group, is much more common among young people than adults. This type of normative gossip is frequently accompanied by teasing.

While adults tremble at the thought of being the target of public gossip and hesitate to admit they gossip, Fine notes, children freely admit they gossip and tease in front of their targets. Even though it can be cruel and hurtful, youngsters say, one learns quickly and directly how to behave acceptably.

Third, gossip has a *reputation effect*. Gossip can both build reputation and also effectively damage it. If having the esteem of one's peer group is significantly important, then guarding against derogatory gossip is of major concern. Children and adults learn quickly that to have power, prestige, and a sterling reputation helps protect them from negative gossip. In a Little League game, for example, high-status team members will usually not be criticized for committing errors, but instead be comforted if they become upset over their poor performance. Low-status players who commit errors, on the other hand, frequently receive insults and scorn, or are ignored by their teammates. Denigrating gossip seems to be primarily directed downward in the social structure. In any case, long before adolescence, children learn to use gossip in managing their own reputations and controlling the reputations of others.

Fourth, because there is an art to gossip, it has an *educational effect*. In learning to gossip adequately, one learns many social skills. Gossiping and hearing oneself being gossiped about helps one develop and maintain poise in embarrassing situations, for example, when in the face of teasing and insults, or when in the presence of others being teased and insulted. Educationally, gossip also develops basic skills of conversation, talking naturally about things that interest us. It also promotes recall ability. To be a successful gossiper, one must be able to recall what others said or what happened.

Sociologists, therefore, are interested in what the neighbors say because their comments and gossip reveal important structures and dynamics of society. Sociologists can help those of us who fear what neighbors might be saying about us by revealing the many positive—socializing, normative, reputational, and educational—effects that neighbor's comments can have in our lives.

CHAPTER 3

The Ways of Conformity: An Approach of Social Psychology

Social psychologists study social influences, asking questions about the effects that groups of people can have on the beliefs and behaviors of others. Sometimes, when they conduct research on the common-sense answers to their questions, they discover that things we're sure are true turn out to be not quite so true when carefully investigated.

For example, most of us would probably believe that, if we overheard someone saying complimentary things about us, we would tend to like that person. And we would be correct. But what researchers Darwyn Linder and Elliot Aranson found equally true was that we tend to like that person *even more* if some comments we overhear them make about us are uncomplimentary. This finding might put a new light on how we feel about negative labels and might make us wonder, then, if a few derogatory words spoken about us now and then by neighbors wouldn't help enhance our likable image among our family, colleagues, and neighbors.

Conformity

For the social psychologist, fear of what the neighbors might say would be categorized as a response to social influence. When, in reaction to this fear, people begin to act in certain socially approved ways in hopes of keeping neighbors from saying uncomplimentary things about them, we say they are socially conforming. For example, as a group of college students came out of a theater, they began saying how much they had liked the film, one after the other praising the experience. The last young woman to speak had actually not enjoyed the film, but under the pressure of her peers' universal approval of the film, she conformed to their opinion and said she also liked it.

Conformity, the response the neighbors desire, may be defined as a change in a person's behavior or attitude as a result of real or imagined pressure from a person or group of people. Because social psychologists realize that people who do crazy things are not necessarily crazy, they are fascinated by the people and situations that can induce many of us normal adults to conform by behaving in ways foreign to our normal self. For example, we all know how quickly groups of rational people can be turned into an angry or frightened mob; how the whispered rumor of a thief can, in moments, transform the emotional tone of a room full of people from merrymaking to terror; how people's firmly held opinions can by swayed when a number of people they admire hold a different opinion; how people who speak with great bravado among their peers seem to lose their confidence in front of bosses or superiors. In each case, the conformity, appearing to be the result of real or imagined pressure by one or more neighbors, becomes grist for the mill of social research.

According to social psychologist Herbert Kelman, social conformity has at least three levels of expression: *compliance, identification,* and *internalization.*

Compliance

Compliance best describes the superficial conformity of people who are motivated by a desire to gain reward or avoid punishment. For example, if we want acquaintances who are normally unfriendly toward us to act in a friendly manner, we may offer to treat them to dinner and a movie as a bribe or reward. Or, if we want our children to be on their best behavior when our guests come, we can either threaten them with a spanking or promise them an ice cream cone. It is common experience that for many compliant people as soon as the reward or punishment ceases so does the desired behavior.

Compliance is what neighbors often induce in us by their threat of disapproval. Compliance, however, is the least enduring expression of conformity and has the least effect on an individual's attitudes and self-image, because people usually comply merely to gain the promised reward or avoid the threatened punishment.

Although rewards and punishments are effective ways of getting people to learn and perform specific activities, they are limited because they must be ever present to have their effect, unless in the meantime the person discovers additional reasons for continuing to perform the approved behavior. An example of continually compliant people are those we call "pleasers." They have developed a habit of quickly and expertly discovering what is expected of them and doing it; the reward they continually seek is that others be pleased with them.

The major factor that brings about the compliant response is *power:* the power of the other person to provide reward for compliance and punishment for noncompliance. The feared neighbors are those who are able to reward me for doing what they want me to do or punish me for refusing to do what they want me to do. Examples of punishment that neighbors mete out to gain compliance include scowls, frowns, derisive laughter, criticism, complaints, refusal to communicate, and the threat that their negative evaluations will be broadcast to others.

Consequently, noncompliance is most often carried out in secret or out of sight and earshot of the feared neighbors. Thus, "Let's not go into this bar because my boss might see us in there" or "Let's park the car a few blocks away, I don't want my parents to notice us together" are ways to avoid possible punishment for behavior that might be labeled noncompliant by certain neighbors. Since compliance has its effects primarily on the level of behavior, it does not usually affect attitudes or beliefs, as do identification and internalization.

Identification

Identification, a second expression of social conformity, describes an imitative response brought about by my desire to be like the neighbors influencing me. Thus, if I admire an individual or a group, I will tend to let myself be influenced by them, not only in my behavior but also in my attitudes and beliefs. I will tend to behave in certain ways like them, think in certain ways like them, and rank my values much as they do, not in order to obtain a reward or avoid punishment (as in compliance) but because I want to be like them. Even though I may not find their behavior or thoughts intrinsically attractive and satisfying, I nevertheless tend to conform because it satisfies my self-image and self-esteem to be in relationship to these persons with whom I identify.

For example, if a young man were to give his girl friend an expensive birthday gift to avoid being called stingy by his peers, he would be acting in *compliance*. If, however, he were giving such a gift because all his chums were accustomed to doing the same and he wanted to be like them, that is, to define himself as one of them, then he would be *identifying*. Although he might come to believe in the quality of generosity his companions valued, his belief would not be very strong, since he would be valuing generosity principally because it was valued by people he found attractive, and not because of any intrinsic reason.

While a compliant person is open to influence from a wide range of neighbors, even unfamiliar and anonymous ones, an identifying person tends to focus his or her attention on a specific set of neighbors, those who affect the person's self-image and self-concept. The reason for this is that the major factor that brings about the identifying response is *attractiveness:* the attractiveness of the neighbors who provide the desirable model.

The persons with whom I identify need not be present physically; all I need is my desire to be like them. So even if the neighbors I admire move away and are not seen by me for years, I am likely to continue to think and act in certain ways, just as I remember them doing.

However, once my model neighbor loses attractiveness in my eyes, or I find other models more attractive than the original, my original behaviors, attitudes, and values may change. For example, Ann admired her father, a powerful executive in a multinational corporation, who felt great antipathy toward social welfare. All through high school she identified with him and proudly parroted his antiwelfare convictions. When she moved away to college, however, she found a group of stimulating friends who, unlike her father, strongly favored social welfare. In a short time, she changed her attitudes toward social welfare *in order to be more like* the new friends she admired.

According to social psychologist Elliot Aronson, if I were an identifier, I would continue to imitate my original models as long as (1) those persons still remained important and attractive to me, (2) they still reported holding the same beliefs, and (3) these beliefs were not challenged by contrary beliefs held by people whom I found more attractive than the original models.

Thus, persons who tend to identify with certain neighbors can be expected to remain true to their original modeling, as Ann did with her father, until other persons appear who are seen as important and more attractive than the original models, as happened to Ann with her college companions.

If you wish to deal successfully with your fear of what the neighbors might say about you, it is important to discover whether you tend to be motivated by compliance, by identification, or by internalization.

Internalization

A third expression of social conformity, the most permanent and most deeply rooted response to social influence, is called *internalization.* The motivation to internalize a particular belief or attitude comes from the desire to be right. When I realize that the persons trying to influence me are trustworthy and of good judgment, and I so accept the truth of the attitude they advocate that I integrate it into my own value system, then internalization has happened. The reward for the belief lies in the inherent truth or rightness of the belief itself. Once an attitude or belief becomes an integral part of my own value system, it enjoys an existence independent of the people who proposed it, and thus becomes extremely resistant to change.

In generating an internalization response, the major factor is *credibility:* the credibility of the person who supplies the new information, belief, or attitude. D. K. Berlo and his associates examined three dimensions of a communicator's credibility: *trustworthiness, expertness,* and *dynamism.* These three vary in importance with different people. For example, among a sample of an adult neighborhood population in Lansing, Michigan, trustworthiness was ranked twice as important as expertness. In contrast, among a college-student sample, trustworthiness and expertness were judged equally important. For both groups, the communicator's dynamism in presenting the new attitude was considered of relatively minor importance.

When we are concerned over the truth of what personally known neighbors might say about us, it is likely that *trustworthiness will be the dominant attribute we look for in a neighbor.* When Katz and Lazarsfeld researched credibility in naturally occurring situations and among familiar neighbors, for example, on the job, in school, and among social groups, they found that trustworthy peers exert considerably more influence than persons of superior status. The importance of trustworthiness is apparently due to continuous contact with peers and friends as compared to periodic contact with authorities and experts. Among the respondents in our research, reported in Part Two, we found that friends in general were considered the most influential neighbors.

F. L. Strodtbeck's research points out, however, that in relationships where there is considerable communication across different levels of status—e.g., children with parents or teachers, adults with bosses or other professionals such as physicians, therapists, lawyers, professors, etc.—superiors, because of their expertness, seem to have greater impact than peers in producing attitude change. In our research, we found that parents in general were considered the most influential cross-status neighbors.

Once we perceive certain neighbors to lack credibility, we are less inclined to listen to what they say about us or be influenced by it. However, when any neighbor makes statements about us regarding a quality that evokes strong ego-involvement, we are likely to scrutinize the truth of what was said. In researching uncomplimentary names people most feared being called by their neighbors, it appeared that certain labels such as "disorganized," "jealous," and "boastful" had low ego-involvement among our respondents, while other labels such as "unfriendly," "incompetent," and "self-centered" evoked high ego-involvement and therefore more fear and concern.

As I begin to be motivated by internalization, that is, to act and think in ways that are true, good, and just, my fear of what the neighbors might say begins to transform. Instead of simply conforming out of desire for approval or threat of disapproval, my concern would probably lead me to begin finding out which neighbors were credible (i.e., expert in the area of their comments about me, and truthful). I would tend to listen to and evaluate the comments of those I found credible. If I perceived the information they offered to be right and true, I would want to change my attitudes and actions accordingly, not because of the neighbors but because of the truthfulness and helpfulness of what they said.

Summary

Any specific action done out of a concern for what the neighbors might say may be due to either compliance, identification, or internalization. For example, suppose at work a notice is posted reminding personnel that coffee breaks are limited to ten minutes. Some workers may comply with the ten-minute regulation because they fear the foreman may be checking on them and would report any violations to the superior. Others who are identifiers may begin returning to their jobs within the ten minutes because their close friends at work do so, and they want to be like them. Still others may have thought about the matter and decided that it is right and just to take only ten minutes. The latter are expressing internalization, that is, listening to their own inner self as neighbor.

Supposing, now, that the foreman is absent for day. The compliant individuals will tend to stretch the length of their coffee breaks, but continue to fear that some other work-neighbor might be spying on them. The identifying individuals will be concerned neither about the foreman spying nor possible punishment from on high; instead, they will tend to keep their eyes focused on the admired neighbors and follow their lead. People who internalized the rule would tend to manifest more flexibility in behavior, neither fearing the foreman's eye nor being overly concerned about what others were doing, but responding to the inner self's choice to act justly, perhaps taking a few minutes less at one break and a few minutes more at another.

Clearly, people who conform primarily out of compliance or identification are most vulnerable to the fear of what the neighbors might say.

CHAPTER 4

Engagement and Disengagement: An Anthropological Perspective

Engaged to the Community

According to anthropologists, a primary function of education, formal and informal, is to lead young human animals to a knowledge of their culture and civilization. Through learning of traditional customs and folkways from a variety of neighbors at home, at school, in church, and at play, these young humans are transformed into members of a specific human culture. In other words, society's first and most essential task is the *engagement of the individual*. This it does by involving young people, directly and indirectly, in its unique living traditions: learning that culture's language observing its laws and etiquette, enjoying its foods, participating in its sports, listening to its music, sharing its myths and visions, wearing its customary clothing, going to its schools, building approved relationships, and finding an acceptable social role.

Individuals quickly learn that clothing, language, behavior, and style of living help give them a clear and well-defined role in the community's dynamics. For example, even as children, we clearly recognize the role of a banker as one who works in a bank, wears a suit, and carries a briefcase; a nurse as one who wears a white uniform and works in a hospital; a physician as one who carries a stethoscope and speaks of disease; a priest as one who wears a roman collar and works in a church.

The first contrast we notice in our response to these socially well-defined people is that we feel comfortable and secure when they are in the places we expect them to be in, dressed the way we expect them to be dressed, and doing the tasks we expect them to be doing—and uncomfortable when they are not.

Everyone in the neighborhood has an investment in keeping everyone else behaving within their expected societal roles. For even though we want to feel free to be different, we want the rest of society to remain predictable, safe, and secure. When people with clearly defined roles are out of place or doing unexpected things, we tend to grow uncomfortable. For example, though I am at ease dealing with department-store salesclerks who help me with a purchase of towels or socks, I would probably feel uncomfortable with a salesclerk who tried to advise me about buying municipal bonds or investing in deferred annuities. And, though I know that nurses could carry out their hospital duties dressed in sweat shirt and jeans, I would feel much more secure being able to walk down a hospital corridor and distinguish nurses from visitors by their white uniforms.

Four Cultural Forces

According to anthropologist Joseph Campbell, we use four cultural forces to keep one another engaged to the community, that is, living according to our culture's norms and social roles.

The first and most obvious cultural force involves *neighbor's comments* or, more precisely, the fear of what the neighbors will say if we don't comply with society's expectations.

The second set of cultural forces keeping us in our place are the *institutions of society*, such as schools, churches, political organizations, family structures, governments, police, and especially the media and the press.

The third cultural force of engagement, a shared inner disposition, is *what we as a society think of as natural and normal.* For example, in the United States people find natural and normal such things as going to class, dating, falling in love, dining in restaurants, eating with knives and forks, buying on credit, celebrating holidays with family, taking vacations, reading newspapers, watching television, and going out on Saturday nights. If, on the other hand, we began driving a car on the left-hand side of the road, eating dinner with our fingers, wearing grass skirts, appearing topless in public, this third cultural force would signal us interiorly that we were behaving in ways most people would consider unnatural or abnormal.

The fourth cultural force keeping us engaged to the community, also a shared inner disposition, is *what we think of as moral and right;* it has to do with values and the meaning of life as seen by our society. In the United States, expressions of this fourth cultural force may be found in the Declaration of Independence, the Bill of Rights, and our system of laws; in the ethical principles enunciated by the medical, legal, psychological professions; in the Ten Commandments and the common teachings of religious denominations. If, in contrast, we began promoting euthanasia, lynching, the abolition of marriage and family life, or the desecration of churches, this fourth inner force would remind us that we were violating the moral expectations of society and that our behavior and thinking was in conflict with the community's shared values and beliefs.

The Strongest and Closest Force

Among all the four forces intent on keeping us living according to cultural expectations, neighbors are the strongest and closest to us. We confront neighbors every day in our homes, on the street, in the store, at the bus stop, in the office. They are the omninpresent and primary enforcers of the social and cultural system. We hear their voices telling us not only what to do and what not to do, but also how, when, and where to do what we do. They tell us how to feel about things, and even why we should be motivated to do what society expects.

Neighbors care very much that we become engaged to society, for without that engagement community life itself is at stake. For this reason, *neighbors speak out not only on their own personal behalf but also on behalf of the other three forces that promote cultural conformity,* namely, the institutions of society, what's natural and normal, and what's moral and right.

As daily enunciators of cultural roles and social customs, neighbors reinforce the patterns and expectations of the *institutions,* for example, by telling us that we ought to think politically the way a certain popular news columnist thinks, we ought to wear clothes like those of a certain soap opera star, or we ought to get married to someone our family approves. By their looks of approval or disapproval, I can tell that my neighbors expect me to think and behave according to the rules and regulations of my family, school, church, government, police, and other social institutions.

What's Natural and Normal

Relatives and friends also model for us what is *natural and normal* and urge us to think, react, and behave according to group norms—sexually, financially, emotionally, religiously, interpersonally.

An extreme example of how neighbors' beliefs of what is natural and normal had disastrous effects occurred during an experiment conducted by psychologist Philip Zimbardo. He hypothesized that, if we were to ask a group of people to think of a prison and how guards in it would naturally and normally behave, chances are most people would imagine prison guards to be tough, callous, unfeeling people, and some people might even label them cruel, tyrannical, and sadistic. If we were to ask people why individuals would become prison guards, some respondents might suggest that the reason is to have an opportunity to exercise their cruelty in a place where their victims could not retaliate.

And what about the prisoners? What kind of people would they be and why might they be in prison? Do you have them pictured as docile, rebellious, plotting escape? No matter. The point is, thanks to our enculturation, we all have inner images and emotions about prison inmates that feel natural and normal, and we sense our perceptions would be shared by many other citizens. One of these shared perceptions would probably be that *both the prisoners and guards are different from us in character and personality.*

Interested in testing some of these perceptions, researcher Philip Zimbardo created a mock prison in the basement of the Psychology Department at Stanford University. Into this prison he brought a group of normal, stable, mature, intelligent young men. By the flip of a coin, Zimbardo designated one half of the group to play the role of prisoners and the other half to play the role of guards. These healthy, normal young men were allowed to live their simulated life as guards and prisoners in a simulated prison for only six days, when Zimbardo was forced to call a halt to the experiment. His own words tell the dramatic story of the power of cultural expectation to transform healthy individuals into frightening personalities.

> At the end of only six days we had to close down our mock prison because what we saw was frightening. It was no longer apparent to us or most of the subjects where they ended and their roles began. The majority had indeed become "prisoners" or "guards," no longer able to clearly differentiate between role-playing and self. There were dramatic changes in virtually every aspect of their behavior, thinking and feeling. In less than a week, the experience of imprisonment undid (temporarily) a lifetime of learning; human values were suspended, self-concepts were challenged, and the ugliest, most base, pathological side of human nature surfaced. We were horrified because we saw some boys ("guards") treat other boys as if they were despicable animals, taking pleasure in cruelty, while other boys ("prisoners") became servile, dehumanized robots who thought only of escape, of their own individual survival, and of their mounting hatred of the guards.

Zimbardo's experiment showed how a strongly internalized cultural force was at work transforming these young men, without any additional influence such as drugs, the promise of reward, or the threat of punishment, into persons who could no longer consciously distinguish between their role playing and their own personalities.

What's Moral and Right

Regarding the fourth cultural force, *what seems moral and right,* many neighbors affirm to us the commonly shared values and meanings of our culture. For example, while among Communists one might be urged to work for the overthrow of the ruling classes, among capitalists one is more likely to be urged to value using one's creative enterprise to earn lots of money and thus become a member of the upper economic class.

At every turn, then, the neighbors are hard at work preserving the social and cultural status quo, keeping everyone in their place, keeping every individual *engaged to the community.* Yet, at a deeper level, a radical change that often confuses us is going on.

Engaged, Disengaged, and Committed

According to anthropologists, beyond the stage of becoming engaged to the community, there appear to be two other stages of cultural maturity during which the neighbors play an important role. In each stage, my relationship to my neighbors is invited to change radically. The names of the three stages of cultural maturity are: *engagement, disengagement,* and *commitment.*

1. Becoming Engaged to the Community

As we have seen, during the first stage, as a young child becoming human, I need to listen to what people around me tell me about myself: who I am, what I should do, how I should respond, what I should value. In this humanizing and socializing process, in learning and integrating the symbols and myths of my community, what the neighbors say is critically important. Without them, I would probably never become socialized, never have a community identity, never truly belong.

I have my neighbors to thank for helping me know my place and giving me a role. They helped me to *fit* into society. I discover that the rules for belonging were established long before I came on the scene. In terms of my personal development, the neighbors helped me to shape a social mask for myself, to create a *persona* with a socially defined role. By doing what neighbors said, I became engaged to the human community.

2. Becoming Disengaged from the Mask

The second stage, *disengagement*, begins when as a young man or woman I wish no longer to be defined simply by the social mask I wear. I wish to move beyond the mask and the well-defined social role to which it confines me, in order to begin becoming a unique individuated human being. I find myself wishing to take the energy I have been investing in developing my persona and now focus it on developing my *self*. I have discovered that, although, during my unconscious childhood, mask making was an essential social development stage, keeping the mask on at all times now stands in the way of my more conscious growth.

Disengagement doesn't always happen, however, because during this second stage I experience two conflicting pressures within me: one toward consciousness, the other toward unconsciousness. The newly felt inner thrust, my movement toward growth and greater consciousness, wants me to loosen the mask I wear, discover my own face, and develop my individual identity. The other inner thrust, which might be called the "neighbors of my childhood" now internalized, prefers that I keep my mask on and remain unconscious.

The inner conflict heightens when I discover I may have given the neighbors (the internalized ones as well as the outer ones) *the right to keep me in my place,* wearing my social mask and behaving in ways they find acceptable and fitting. As a rule, I discover, neighbors prefer to deal with me when I am wearing my mask and playing an accepted role with which they feel comfortable and secure. This observation received strong support from the research of Stanley Schacter, who showed that the persons who were liked most were those who most conformed to the group norm. Deviates and non-conformists were liked *least*. It has also been noted that neighbors tend to be most comfortable seeing me in a single mask and resist changing their social perception of me. For instance, my parents have always viewed me in the role of a child and have difficulty seeing me as an adult professional. And my children prefer to see me simply as their parent and resist dealing with the complexity of my many roles. Among the neighbors, the general wish is that I remain consistent, predictable, easy to understand and deal with.

During this second stage of cultural maturity, many of us reject the challenge of disengagement and simply acquiesce to the spoken or felt expectations of the neighbors. Fear of the neighbor's disapproval often robs us of the ability to discern and act on our own true values, wants, and rights. Besides, we find that this path of least resistance is also the path of widest social acceptance. We find ourselves well rewarded by neighborly approval for continuing to be good boys and nice girls.

Those who follow this accepted path serve society by keeping its wheels lubricated and preserving the *status quo*. But, in the end, they remain at the mercy of what the neighbors say, and must stifle the thrust of the inner voice that really knows them and would guide them to greater consciousness and self-actualization.

The Third Radical Change

3. Engaging My Community: Commitment

There is an alternative path that follows the thrust of my inner wisdom, which also serves the community but in a different way. After disengaging myself from the image/mask the neighbors would have me wear permanently, the inner thrust invites me to make a conscious commitment to serve the community in the light of wider human values and visions.

The capacity of any culture's vision to grow and evolve depends to a great extent on courageous individuals who disengage themselves from the culture in order to enrich it with new ideas, myths, and perceptions. Such individualists (nonconformists, innovators, misfits, and deviates) are usually not appreciated by society until well after they are dead and buried. While they are alive, as John F. Kennedy showed in his book *Profiles in Courage*, a series of biographies of innovative Americans, such individualists usually meet strongest resistance from the people to whose demands they refuse to conform. Kennedy himself felt those pressures to conformity in the United States Senate. In the introduction to his book, he wrote:

> Americans want to be liked—and senators are no exception. . . . We enjoy the comradeship and approval of our friends and colleagues. We prefer praise to abuse, popularity to contempt. . . . We realize, moreover, that our influence in the club—and the extent to which we can accomplish our objectives and those of our constituents—are dependent in some measure on the esteem with which we are regarded by the other senators. "The way to get along," I was told when I entered Congress, "is to go along."

When, therefore, I wish to commit myself not to preserving the status quo but to challenging the community's vision, I open myself up to misunderstanding and even abuse from my neighbors. In making a commitment to the community, I am invited to live and work from out of my inner self. In answering this call to a third radical change in my relationship to my neighbors, I do not discard my social roles but rather integrate them into a more conscious alternative pathway of human service. As a conscious adult, I would no longer be tied to my community *out of fear* that my safety and security might be taken away by what the neighbors might say. Rather, out of love for those same neighbors, I would commit myself to call them forth to greater consciousness and growth.

CHAPTER 5

The Mirror of Neighbors: A Psychological Perspective

For the psychologist, experiences that happened during childhood, when my budding ego was taking shape, are very important for understanding how I respond today to what the neighbors might say about me. The dynamics of human development and the related experiences of self-image and self-esteem offer an important psychological perspective to our study.

Mirroring and Self-Image

Each of us carries around our own image of who we are, and this sense of self often governs our reactions and behavior. A self-image may or may not be realistic: a highly attractive-looking person may have a sense of being unattractive; a bright person in a family of very bright persons may be convinced he or she is dull and stupid.

My self-image is a summary of my experiences of myself. It includes an image of my body as large or small, dexterous or clumsy, beautiful or ugly. It includes an image of my intelligence, emotions, creativity, motives, and so on. Even my personal decisions tend to reflect my self-image. If I perceive myself as stupid, I will tend to avoid intellectual challenges, even though mental tests show me to be of superior intelligence. If you perceive yourself as clumsy, you will expect to fail on tasks requiring manual skill or graceful and controlled movements, and you probably have a history of such failures.

According to psychologists Ross Stagner and Charles M. Solley, people who do not live up to their potential are likely to be individuals with self-images distorted by unfortunate experiences during childhood. Conversely, they state, persons who achieve more than would be predicted from their abilities alone are usually those who at an early age acquired an image of themselves as competent and successful.

The question is: How did my self-image get to be the way it is?

There are many answers to that question. One important answer is that the neighbors, especially my parents, provided the first psychological mirror in which I could see myself.

I know that, physically, I cannot see my own image without the aid of a mirroring surface, and that the image reflected by a bathroom mirror is much more true than the distortion of my face reflected by the surface of a pond or a shiny doorknob. In a similar way, according to psychiatrist Heinz Kohut in his book *The Restoration of the Self* and psychiatrist Jacques Lacan in his book *The Language of the Self,* I also need a psychological mirror in order to develop a self-image. Both theorists agree that my mother's mirroring of me generated the most significant reflections and that my father's mirroring came next in importance. If I had parents as realistically reflective of me as the bathroom mirror, parents who reflected me in an approving, positive light, I am more likely to have a healthy self-image and strong self-esteem than if I had parents who reflected me in a negative and distorted way. Thus, if today I perceive myself as stupid and you image yourself as clumsy, it is likely that we had parents who by their words or behavior reflected to some degree an image of us as stupid or clumsy.

In general, my mother and father mirrored me by their words, feelings, and behavior toward me. As they reflected more and more of what they perceived me to be, I slowly developed a summary sense of myself. Most studies agree that the self-image takes firm shape during early childhood.

Congruency

As I grew older, getting feedback from significant people in the outside world about how they saw me and experienced me was a continuous mirroring process. Out of that process—hearing the verbal and nonverbal messages that I was friendly, likable, generous, etc.—I began to put together an image of myself as friendly, likable, generous, etc. I began to develop a sense of myself as the world saw me. I heard people acting and talking as if I were someone who was intelligent, worth listening to, a good companion; and I began to shape a self-image congruent with the image of me mirrored by my parents and other important neighbors.

Congruency is an important element in developing a healthy self-image. For example, it would be difficult for me to continue thinking of myself as an intelligent person if in many ways, verbal and nonverbal, I began getting messages from people around me at school and work that they did not perceive me as intelligent. In order to maintain an image of myself as intelligent in spite of much feedback to the contrary, I would need to have "intelligent" as a firmly developed part of my self-image, probably from early childhood.

Because people often do not have a strong, positive sense of self, they are very easily led to question the positive aspects of their self-image. In contrast, negative aspects of a self-image are often firmly maintained. A frequent task in psychotherapy is to reverse, remove, or replace erroneous self-perceptions. For example, if I see myself as incompetent, although tests show I am quite competent, a psychotherapist can mirror my competencies to me, enabling me to gain a more accurate self-image.

During childhood, we are led to trust our own parents to reflect who we are honestly and accurately, primarily because they are the persons we also trust to provide us with nurturing and protection. Unfortunately, certain parents reflect their children as ugly, stupid, boring, inadequate, unlovable, and a whole host of other unwelcome labels, probably not consciously but subtly, yet effectively enough for such self-perceptions to last through adulthood. This is what happened to Karen.

As a child, Karen would begin chattering away as soon as she opened the kitchen door after school. But she remembered how her mother continually put down her chattiness with comments such as, "Can't you see I'm busy now?" or "Why don't you go out and play?" The *message* Karen heard in these comments was "I'm not interested in you. I'm bored with what you're saying." Consequently, Karen began to image herself as a boring person, not as someone others would listen to or be interested in. Her parents, the ones from whom she most needed positive feedback at an early age, were effectively undermining her self-confidence in relationships. Karen gradually became quiet, shy, and noncontributing in conversations. Finally, she generalized her parents' original indifference toward her to the whole world's indifference and learned to find confirmations of that negative self-image in the reflections of other neighbors.

Therapeutically, Karen's task was to become conscious that certain neighbors *were* offering her other, positive reflections that she could use to shape a healthier self-image and begin the slow but rewarding work of revisioning herself.

To the degree that we understand and accept the self-image we have now, are we able to envision our self-image in a new way and begin to transform it. The poet W. H. Auden once observed that a person cannot begin the process of transformation "unless he first chooses himself as he is now with all his finite limitations. To reach the 'age of consent' means to arrive at the point where the 'given' ego-self relationship is changed into a contractual one." Reaching maturity means we are no longer simply shaped by the "given" circumstances, but we can draw up a self-contract to begin assuming responsibility for changing the image we currently have of ourselves. Revisioning is the transformative task, and it begins within.

Inner and Outer Neighbors

From a psychological perspective, neighbors are in great part *internalized people.* The most important of these inner neighbors are my internalized parents. During those impressionable first years, I so repeatedly heard the ways my parents described me that I mentally recorded their messages about me and can play those recordings back for myself at any time, even when my parents are absent. So I really don't have to ask, "I wonder what my parents would say?" because I already know.

It may seem that during childhood I also internalized the messages of other relatives and neighbors, but some psychologists would say that it is probably more accurate to say that what I internalized was not what the neighbors themselves were saying but *what my parents told me the neighbors were feeling and saying about me,* that is, my parents' projection onto these neighbors. In one sense, then, for the child all neighbors are ultimately, if unconsciously, facets of the internalized parents. During childhood we learn to identify the projections our parents make upon the neighbors in at least three ways: we hear or overhear some, we intuit others, and still others are picked up through watching our parents' behavioral reactions. The labels we most fear being given seem to be those that have been reinforced in all three ways.

During childhood Marybel had built up a large collection of paper dolls, which she treasured. When her friend Cindy came over they played together for hours with the paper dolls, making up their own dramas. These cutouts represented a rich and highly valued imaginal world for Marybel and an opportunity for exercising her own dramatic creativity. She continued the story:

> One day Cindy said to me in front of my mother that she would like to have some of my paper dolls. She may have even offered to buy them. I don't remember. I know I didn't want to give them to her or even sell them to her because I knew nothing got cared for at her house. She had a batch of brothers and sisters who were forever going through her

> toys, and I probably imagined my paper dolls would get lost or destroyed. Even more, I didn't want to give up these treasured possessions because I had carefully selected them and bought them with my own money. My mother, however, said I was selfish and stingy not to give some paper dolls to Cindy. As far as my mother was concerned, I had more of them than I needed, and she insisted I give some to Cindy.
>
> I can't remember if I actually gave her any paper dolls. That wasn't important. The damage that was done was that I was labeled as stingy and selfish. Not only did my mother name me so, but this indelible naming was witnessed by my friend (and projected onto her) so that the message became, "Cindy also sees you as selfish and stingy."

In that example, the projection was clearly *heard.* Marybel told of another incident where her mother's projection onto the neighbors was *intuited.*

> One Saturday afternoon, Cindy and I were playing dress-up, and we went outside in our dress-up clothes. I was wearing a straw, pancake-shaped hat with blue ribbons for tying under the chin. Later when I came in the house, I was greeted by my mother with, "Your Aunt Miriam called to tell me she saw you on the street with that stupid, ridiculous-looking hat on your head." She didn't say it, but her unspoken message to me was, "Everybody in the neighborhood sees you as ridiculous and stupid. Don't you know any better than to make a public fool of yourself and shame the whole family?"

Marybel's mother's embarrassment also showed in her physical reactions when she threatened to throw away the offending hat.

Events like these had a destructive effect on Marybel's self-image. As she put it, "When I began to realize I was capable of embarrassing my mother and my family without even knowing it, I wondered how I could ever again trust my creative, playful side not to present me as ridiculous, thus embarrassing me and all those who are important to me. So I pushed my playful and creative side down under for fear it would be noticed and get me in trouble again."

Fear and Trust

Fear of what the neighbors might say is often precisely that: *fear*. The word *fear*, of course, may refer to a continuum of emotional responses. Sometimes our fear is found on the weaker end of the continuum and might better be described as dislike, concern, annoyance, or bother; but for certain people at certain times, their fear is stronger and may rightfully be described as anxiety, or even terror.

Why do we fear our neighbors rather than trust them? What keeps us from having what Erik Erikson called a *basic trust* in our neighbors?

To answer this question, psychologists such as Erikson and Abraham Maslow point again to early childhood experience, for they believe that a sense of security in the world and trust in people happens (or does not happen) at an early age. Thus, if during infancy I experience much discomfort, tension, and long delays in having my everyday needs met, I may well acquire an image of the outside world as withholding satisfaction, threatening, and hostile; of my parents as neglectful or rejecting of me; and of myself as helpless, mistreated, and perhaps not very valuable. Conversely, if during infancy I encounter relatively few threats and am nurtured, cuddled, protected, and comforted by my parents, my image of the world, my parents, and myself will be very different. I will probably develop an attitude of basic trust, experience people as good and caring, and see the world as an interesting and rewarding place.

Children who develop a sense of the world as hostile, threatening, and unable to satisfy their needs seem more likely to respond with fear at the thought of what neighbors might say than children having basic trust. Just as trusting persons tend to feel confident that others will like them, untrusting persons tend to feel certain they will not be liked.

According to psychologist Abraham Maslow, every child has a certain set of primary needs, the satisfaction of which is crucial in developing a sense of basic trust. These primary needs in their order of appearance in a child's life are: *phys-*

iological needs (food, drink, clothing, warmth, touch, etc.), *security needs* (feeling safe, protected, nonthreatened, and knowing parents will quickly come to the rescue if there is danger or some serious problem), *belongingness needs* (feeling wanted, welcomed, loved, cared for, a part of the family), and *esteem needs* (feeling valued, respected, listened to, taken into consideration, affirmed, etc.). Maslow lists a fifth level of needs, *self-actualization needs*, which usually appears only when the other four primary needs are being met.

Children who consistently fail to have their primary needs adequately satisfied are not likely to develop basic trust either toward the outside world or toward themselves. If you are strongly affected by fear of what the neighbors might say about you, check back to see if some of your primary needs were denied or went woefully unfulfilled during childhood. Early feelings of insecurity, anxiety, pessimism, and mistrust often remain with us throughout life, and help account for the times when we are motivated by fear.

In contrast, when basic needs are continually being provided for, a strong ego can develop, an ego that can then be free to work on self-actualization needs.

Self-Image and Cumulative Experience

In addition to those who say a person's capacity to trust others is largely determined in early life, especially by the parental style of caring, there are those like clinical psychologist Julian Rotter of the University of Connecticut who believe that the inclination to trust or distrust is probably learned over a longer period of time, and that it results from a person's cumulative experiences. Furthermore, they say, such trust is not an all-or-nothing thing, since persons usually do not trust or distrust all others equally. For example, while I might distrust women because of a series of unfortunate experiences during adolescence, I may still trust my own mother and the women in my family, believing they are exceptions to the rule.

To persons who would like to change their fear of what neighbors might say into an attitude of trust, Rotter's studies are helpful and encouraging. They show that low trusters can learn to be more trusting, if they really want to, simply by *practicing.* "If somebody says something to you which you disbelieve without any evidence," suggests Rotter, "act as if you believe it and see what happens." Rotter claims to have become a high truster this way.

Although one might suspect that highly trusting people would be a gullible lot and ripe targets for con artists, Rotter's research shows just the opposite. For example, it's the low trusters who are the usual victims of con artists and their games. It's the low trusters who are perceived by others as less trustworthy—and are actually more likely than high trusters to lie, steal, and cheat. In contrast, the evidence shows that highly trusting people are seen by others as trustworthy. Moreover, as a group they are, reportedly, also happier and perceived by their neighbors as more likable, and are sought after more often as friends by both low-trusting and high-trusting people.

Rotter acknowledges that highly trusting people tend to have parents who model and teach trust. Unfortunately, he said, many families teach *distrust.*

A sense of basic distrust naturally makes people fearful and suspicious of what neighbors might say. When low trusters also begin trying to deal with their inner-neighbor voices, confusion is added to their fear and suspicions.

The Reality of the Interpersonal

Although the influence of parents on us is critically powerful, there are others who can and do touch us in significant ways, even during childhood. Echoing Julian Rotter's claim about the power of cumulative experience in developing the ability to trust, psychologist James Youniss has uncovered an important role friends play in a child's self-image as a moral person. Without denying the importance of parents and other adults in the moral development of children, Youniss claims that "critical discussions which children have with peers and friends are an equally important source for moral decisions."

Such peer discussions, he said, "are the basis for cooperation and mutual respect—two attitudes which are rarely achieved in parent-child exchanges because the parent is the superior agent in the exchange. But children arrive at interactions on an equal footing with their peers and can seek a cooperative relationship without fear of losing self to a superior agent." Following in the footsteps of developmental psychologist Jean Piaget and interpersonal psychiatrist Harry Stack Sullivan, Youniss says his research suggests that *interdependence*, rather than either unilateral coercion by parents or individual, independent, rational thinking, is the mature mode of decision making in important and personal matters.

According to the results of our questionnaire, respondents in general named "friends" as the most significant and influential neighbors in their lives, suggesting that Youniss's model of mutual interdependence is the preferred mode for certain adult decision making. Therefore, although the influence of parents on us is crucial, and although we must each assume responsibility for our inner psychological work and our own life, it is clear that most of our qualities can be developed, most of our needs can be satisfied, and most of our important decisions can be made *only in relationship to others*, the outer neighbors. Before we look at these outer neighbors and how we perceive them, there is one other element to explore: what has been traditionally called *conscience*, or the voice of the soul.

The Role of Conscience

The voice of conscience comes from the deepest core of the self. It is not an internalized parental or neighbor message, though its voice sometimes concurs with such a message. Conscience may be distinguished from inner parents and inner neighbors in at least four ways.

First, internalized parents' and neighbors' messages usually come in generalities such as "You should always do this" or "You must never say that." Words like *always, never, should,* and *must* signal the presence of inner parents and inner neighbors. The true self's voice usually speaks to precise, actual situations and tries to tell me a truth about myself. Conscience's comments might sound like "That really was a low blow you dealt him" or "You were really trying to sneak in an ulterior message with that comment, weren't you?"

Second, whereas inner parents and neighbors often try to evoke fear or anxiety in me and otherwise immobilize my ability to think and act in my best interests, my inner self's conscience moves me to insight, intuition, and a place of inner peace from which a clear decision to act may be made.

Third, though inner parents and neighbors call me to conformity without question, the inner self will ask many questions in an effort to bring me to fuller consciousness concerning who I am and what I am called to do in the world during my lifetime.

Fourth, inner parents and neighbors usually want me not to disturb the status quo but to go along with everyone else. My conscience, however, may point to awareness of a felt desire to "follow a road less traveled" and challenge me to explore that awareness and to follow it if it seems right for me. Sometimes such calls and challenges to engage the community are voiced by a real neighbor outside me. When this happens, inner neighbors usually want me to disregard the call and follow the secure path, but conscience confronts me with the call that has been voiced and asks me to discern whether or not it is a part of my truth.

Summary

Now that we begin to understand some of the dynamics—psychological, sociological, and anthropological—that help explain our fear of what neighbors might say about us, let us examine some of the labels that people today actually fear.

PART TWO

The Labels People Fear

What qualities or labels do people today fear might be applied to them by others? To find out, we presented a questionnaire to more than four hundred men and women, all of whom lived in the Middle Atlantic states, mostly along the Boston–Washington, D.C., corridor.

Respondents fell into four age groups; high school, college, young adults (ages twenty-three to forty), and those over forty years of age. Age and sex were the only identifying characteristics respondents were asked to give.

In the questionnaire we asked respondents to rank the labels they most feared. The first set of labels to be ranked viewed the respondent as a *relating person*. These labels include impolite, unfriendly, unattractive, disliked, ungrateful, and jealous. Viewing the respondent as a *competent person*, the second set of labels included stupid, a failure, disorganized, incompetent, irresponsible, and a "bad" parent, child, friend, worker, etc. The third set focused on the respondent's *inner qualities* and included eight labels: cruel, stingy, superficial, lazy, immoral, boastful, self-centered, and phony.

In each category, respondents were invited to write in other labels that were of special personal concern, but only about 5 percent felt a need to do so. Most found that the questionnaire's checklist of labels satisfied their needs.

In each category, we asked respondents to rank the labels they feared most—first, second, and third. Psychologically, although it is impossible to specify what it might mean for respondents to rank this or that label as the one they fear most, it is likely that no matter which label they choose they are motivated by a major underlying concern: *What will happen to me?* People are concerned about the personal consequences of being labeled negatively. Will they be hurt? Will they be disapproved? Will they be abandoned?

In the following four chapters we explore in turn those labels of relating, competency, and inner qualities about which people worry most. Not surprisingly, men and women in different age groups respond more strongly to some labels than to others.

Before discussing the labels, let's examine the different neighbors whose opinions most influence people. Who are the people respondents most frequently mention as having the power to make them self-conscious, influence the way they live, or even change their minds about an important decision?

CHAPTER 6

Who Is My Neighbor?

It was never our intention to restrict an understanding of the term *neighbors* to the people who live next door or down the street.

Once, when Jesus was discussing the divine commandment "Thou shalt love thy neighbor as thyself," a Pharisee interrupted him with the question "But who is my neighbor?" Jesus replied by telling the parable of the Good Samaritan who caringly intervened in the life of an abandoned stranger.

Like Jesus, we understand neighbors as those who cross our path and influence our choices, actions, and ultimately our lives. Our neighbors are the persons we listen to. We notice what they say. Whether we love them, fear them, or both, their words and actions have an impact on us.

Consider those people whose opinion or judgment you take into consideration when making a choice to do or not do something. Those are your neighbors.

In our questionnaire, we asked respondents to check off, from a list of ten likely neighbors, the ones whose opinions significantly influence them. Respondents were allowed to check as many neighbor categories as they liked and invited to write in influential others not on our list. The average number of responses in this part of the questionnaire were about three per person. Both men and women had the same average number of significant-neighbor categories.

Despite interesting variations among different age groups,

there was a clear consensus about the highest-ranking influential neighbors among our total sample.

Both men and women ranked their most important neighbors in the same order: friends first, mothers second, and fathers third. According to Figure 1, after the first three ranked categories, the percentage of response drops off significantly.

Let us examine each of the neighbor categories in order.

Figure 1
MOST INFLUENTIAL NEIGHBORS RANKED
(total sample N=429)

Rank	Category	Percent Marking this Category
1	Friends	63
2	Mother	59
3	Father	45
4	Schoolmates	20
5	Workmates	18
6	Spouse (including girl friends and boyfriends)	17
7	Sister(s)	15
8	Brother(s)	14
9	Next-Door Neighbors	6
10	Others	6

Friends

According to our sample, friends are the most influential neighbors overall, both for men and women in general. However, there are some interesting exceptions, as can be seen from Tables A-1 and A-2 in the Appendix.

For example, among high school girls and young adult women between the ages of twenty-three and forty, "friends" played second fiddle to "mother" in frequency of influence. Among our respondents, it was men in general, college women, and women over forty who seemed most to give "friends" the power to influence their decisions and self-image.

Although the questionnaire did not ask respondents to specify what friends they meant, it is likely that some friends were also schoolmates or workmates. Some respondents checked all three categories—friends, workmates, schoolmates—but it is not certain whether these three are independent categories or not.

That friends are the most frequently mentioned determiners of influence seems a healthy sign, for as a rule friends who care about us are most likely to speak words about us worth listening to.

It is interesting to compare the influence of friends and spouses (including girl friends and boyfriends).

Except among young adult women where influence of spouse is strongest (35 percent), every other group in Figure 2 rates friends' influence at least twice as high as that of the spouses.

Figure 2
COMPARISON OF FRIEND AND SPOUSE CATEGORIES AMONG ADULTS
(percent marking each category)

Category	Young Adult Women	Women over Forty	Young Adult Men	Men over Forty
Friends	60%	56%	52%	49%
Spouse (including girl friend and boyfriend)	35%	27%	24%	23%

Mother

Certainly the most controversial neighbor and the one most written about as an influence in our lives and choices is mother.

According to Figure 3, mothers seem to have their highest impact among the high school girls in our sample. Eight out

Figure 3
COMPARING MOTHER AND FRIENDS
INFLUENCE AMONG WOMEN
(percent marking each category)

Category	High School Girls	College Females	Young Adult Women	Women over Forty
Mother	81%	72%	64%	29%
Friends	71%	76%	60%	56%

of ten of these girls saw their mother as a powerful influence. During women's college years, the influence of mother drops in frequency to second place, with "friends" becoming the most influential (76 percent). However, among young adult women, mother's influence returns to first place until the over-forty period.

Figure 4
COMPARING MOTHER INFLUENCE
BETWEEN WOMEN AND MEN
(percent marking Mother category)

Category	High School	College Age	Young Adult	Over Forty	Average
Females	81%	72%	64%	29%	65%
Males	59%	61%	66%	21%	53%

Though the overall frequency of mother's influence is stronger among women than men in our sample, mother's influence among men reaches its peak during the young adult years. Two out of three male respondents aged twenty-three to forty marked mother as an influential neighbor.

Father

In our sample, fathers were most frequently mentioned as influential neighbors by high school boys and girls. Almost two out of every three of these adolescents marked father as a neighbor to whom they listen and whose disapproval they fear. As is clear from Figure 5, fathers remain a consistently significant influence in all groups under forty years of age, and third in rank overall in our sample.

Figure 5
CHOOSING FATHER AS A SIGNIFICANT NEIGHBOR
(percent marking Father category)

Category	High School	College Age	Young Adult	Over Forty	Average
Females	66%	49%	36%	19%	44%
Males	63%	56%	50%	12%	46%

Naturally, many respondents marked both mother and father as influential and powerful neighbors. However, from the statistics we cannot tell which respondents perceived mother and father together as a single neighbor unit and which perceived them independently.

Primary Neighbors

We did not present the questionnaire to children younger than high school age, so we do not have any statistical data on those whom children consider their most influential neighbors. However, we can extrapolate from psychological research that the primary family exerts the most frequent and powerful influence during this period. For the child, the immediate family remains the most important neighbor, the most feared critic whose voice rings loudest, often drowning out all other voices that would speak a different view of reality.

Spouses, Boyfriends, and Girl Friends

Although the category of spouse or primary relational partner was not included in the questionnaire's checklist of neighbors, it received significant write-in response, so much so that when we totaled all the handwritten entries that represented a primary relational partner—wife, husband, fiancé, boyfriend, girl friend, lover, live-in, etc.—this category, which we labeled "spouse," ranked sixth highest overall in our sample.

Figure 6
COMPARING MALE AND FEMALE RESPONSE TO SPOUSE CATEGORY
(percent marking Spouse category)

Category	High School	College Age	Young Adult	Over Forty	Average
Females	6%	10%	35%	27%	18%
Males	6%	5%	24%	23%	16%

There is reason to believe that this category is more influential than it is statistically represented here. First, write-in responses require that a respondent not merely make a check mark in a box, but consciously specify in writing a new category. Our presumption is that had there been a "spouse" category to check, many would have done so. Second, the "spouse" category does not receive much attention from our respondents until after college; from then on, more than one out of every four adult respondents wrote in an entry that we included under "spouse." It is safe to say that at least as many of our high school and college respondents were influenced in their choices and decisions by special boyfriends and girl friends. Therefore, we can presume these younger people must have included such primary partners under the "friends" category.

When we rank the influence of spouses and other primary-partner categories upon those over forty in our sample, we see that "spouse" influence ranks third for this group. Among women over forty, only "friends" and "mother" seem to have more frequent or powerful influence than spouses. Among men over forty, only "workmates" and "friends" surpass the influence of spouses in frequency. However, as already noted,

Figure 7
COMPARING RANKS OF INFLUENTIAL NEIGHBORS FOR MALE AND FEMALE ADULTS OVER FORTY

Rank	Female	Male
1	Friends	Workmates
2	Mother	Friends
3	Spouse (including boyfriend)	Spouse (including girl friend)
4	Workmates	Mother
5	Father	Father

the category "spouse" was a write-in response. Therefore, it probably carries more significance than represented in our questionnaire results and may indeed deserve a rank higher than third.

Workmates and Schoolmates

Among our general sample, schoolmates and workmates, who ranked fourth and fifth in importance, respectively, provide an interesting group of neighbors to study.

For example, males in general seem to be influenced by their peers at school and on the job about twice as much as females in general.

Possibly because traditionally men are taught to value competition, productivity, and success, they are much more conscious than women of the opinions of people on the job and

Figure 8
COMPARING MALE AND FEMALE RESPONSE TO SCHOOLMATES AND WORKMATES CATEGORIES
(percent marking each category)

Category	Schoolmates	Workmates
Males	21%	25%
Females	11%	12%

in class. It may also be true that men more than women tend to cultivate friendships around schoolwork and shoptalk, and so tend to connect their friends with school and work.

Perhaps, in contrast, females tend to make clearer distinctions between neighbors they perceive as friends and those they deal with at work and school, even when these workmates and schoolmates may be the very same persons they call friends.

Figure 9
COMPARING MALE AND FEMALE RESPONSE TO WORKMATES AS INFLUENTIAL NEIGHBORS
(percent marking Workmates category)

Category	High School	College Age	Young Adults	Over Forty	Average
Males	13%	20%	20%	51%	25%
Females	4%	5%	20%	27%	12%

Only among the young adults in our sample did men and women mark their workmates with equal frequency.

Sisters and Brothers

According to Figure 10, females tend to be more sensitive to the comments of their own sisters (fourth rank) than to their brothers (sixth rank), while males tend to be more conscious of comments coming from their brothers (seventh rank) than from their sisters (ninth rank).

It may be important here to note that the influence of older siblings is usually most strongly felt during childhood, years that were not measured in our survey. So, despite low frequency of sibling influence among our sample, we would urge you not to dismiss brothers and sisters as a significant factor in shaping a view of yourself. The fact may be that long before now you internalized and integrated the opinions and judgments of your sisters and brothers into your own inner neighbor.

Figure 10
COMPARING RANKS OF INFLUENTIAL NEIGHBORS FOR FEMALES AND MALES

Rank	Females	Males
1	Friends	Friends
2	Mother	Mother
3	Father	Father
4	Sister(s)	Workmates
5	Husband (including boyfriend)	Schoolmates
6	Brother(s)	Wife (including girl friend)
7	Workmates	Brother(s)
8	Schoolmates	Other Relatives
9	Other Relatives	Sister(s)
10	Others	Neighbors

Other Categories

The vague category "other relatives" was marked by one out of eight respondents. We have no way of telling whether their check marks indicated aunts, uncles, cousins, grandparents, in-laws, or some other relatives. Some of the case stories in the following chapters may help clarify how the constellation of other relatives influences choices people make.

Among our sample, the questionnaire category "neighbors," comprising the people who "live next door," "on our street," or "in our apartment building," received almost no notice from the younger people.

If any of our respondents seemed concerned about what was being said over backyard fences or in apartment building hallways, it would be the over-forty age group. Evidently, they are the only generation who seem concerned with what people in their neighborhood say about them, even when such neighbors are neither family, friends, nor workmates.

"Children," another write-in category, was mentioned no-

Figure 11
COMPARING INFLUENCE OF NEXT-DOOR NEIGHBORS AMONG MALE AND FEMALE RESPONDENTS
(percent marking Neighbor category)

Category	High School	College Age	Young Adults	Over Forty	Average
Females	4%	2%	7%	10%	5%
Males	6%	5%	6%	9%	7%

ticeably only by women over forty. One in seven such women wrote "children" in the blank space provided by the questionnaire. "Children" may have had an even more significant influence among our sample, since children would qualify in the "other relatives" category.

It may be of interest to mention some of the other write-in categories. At every age level, a few respondents referred to themselves having *inner neighbors*. Again, at every age level, a few mentioned being influenced by people connected with their church or religion, for example, "clergy," "female parishioners," "my religious community," "church peers who are not clergy," or "the church and people associated with it."

Except for one woman in the over-forty group, only men respondents wrote in authority figures such as bosses, supervisors, or teachers.

One older male respondent wrote in, "The new neighbor is television!"

Now that we have a sense of who today's influential neighbors are, we can begin to explore some of the labels about which people are most concerned.

CHAPTER 7

Relating Labels People Fear

People concerned about how they relate to others wonder, "Am I seen as polite or impolite, attractive or unattractive, grateful or ungrateful, friendly or unfriendly?"

How do people come to fear some labels more than others? What makes people worry about one label but not another? How can people learn to deal with fears of what neighbors might say?

Some of our questionnaire respondents felt *fear* was too strong a word, preferring expressions such as *don't like* or *uncomfortable with*. Nevertheless, whether a person's precise response is fear or dislike, both are unwelcome feelings and both are triggered by the thought that other people may be labeling us in a negative way.

Figure 12 shows how our respondents in general ranked their fears about relating labels. We weighed their first choice highest (three points), their second choice next highest (two points), and their third least high (one point).

Compared to the strong concern respondents expressed about the labels "unfriendly" and "disliked," their concern for other labels in this group falls significantly lower. There are no significant differences in ranking of relating labels between men and women.

We will consider some meanings and implications for all six labels, since for certain people even the less popularly feared

Figure 12
SUMMARY RANKING OF RELATING LABELS FEARED
(total sample N=429)

Rank	Label	Weighted Score
1	Unfriendly	234
2	Disliked	220
3	Ungrateful	117
4	Unattractive	97
5	Impolite	92
6	Jealous	40

labels can have a powerful impact. Table A-3 in the Appendix summarizes questionnaire results regarding relating labels.

1. Unfriendly

In general, our respondents ranked "unfriendly" the most feared of all relating labels. More specifically, being called unfriendly seems to be of primary concern to high school students, both boys and girls. Although in our college sample men seemed more concerned about this label than women, the focus shifts to women among the adult respondents. In our sample, every single woman over forty marked "unfriendly" as one of her first, second, or third most feared relating labels.

"I wonder how often I have feared being seen as unfriendly," said one woman over forty, "when I didn't feel like

Figure 13
COMPARISON OF RESPONSE TO "UNFRIENDLY" CATEGORY BETWEEN FEMALES AND MALES
(weighted scores given)

Category	High School	College Age	Young Adults	Over Forty	Total
Females	30	24	28	41	123
Males	27	30	25	29	111

being as open, talkative, or affectionate as someone indicated they would like me to be."

"I fear people in the office will see me as unfriendly," said a young executive, "when I'm in a hurry and don't stop to talk, or I cut people short. Yet I have to because I'm rushed."

"Sometimes when I feel moody and disagreeable I avoid chatting with people," said a college-dorm resident, "but I'm afraid they will talk about me and say I'm an unfriendly person."

"I've had men accuse me of being aloof and unfriendly," said a young woman, "because I didn't welcome their sexual advances." A woman standing next to her added, "I have a similar problem with a man in our office. I end up feeling unfriendly because I feel *I have to be unfriendly* in order to stop his unwelcome advances."

Laura, a teenager in psychotherapy, admitted she often presented a smiling face to people while internally she was criticizing and disliking them. She lived in fear that people would see the real, critical her, so she tried even harder to appear friendly. Since she felt she was acting deceptively, she couldn't let herself believe that others were speaking truthfully when they said they liked her. In therapy, Laura learned to discriminate between what was inside her and what was coming from the outside. She needed to learn to say no and know that was acceptable. She needed to learn it was all right not to like certain people.

The "unfriendly" label is one that is often feared from childhood. Typically, it is a fear passed on to children by parents. One parent told us a story about planting this fear in her own daughter's mind.

> Debbie had one of her first-grade friends over to our house but didn't want to play with her. Debbie was in a bad mood. When she resisted playing, I got overconcerned and angry at her. I took her out of the room where she had been with her friend, but probably not out of earshot, and told her if she wasn't friendly, nobody would like her and she wouldn't have any friends. "So, be friendly," I said. "Go back in the room and be nice."

As we later found out, the mother's anger came out of her own childhood fears of being seen as unfriendly. The mother continued her story.

> Debbie's friend seemed to have overheard my words, and began to treat Debbie as if she were unfriendly. To Debbie, my words acted like a prophecy, because from then on she began to fear that what I had predicted about her was true.

In talking with this mother, we discovered both she and her daughter had an inner neighbor who often reminded them, "Be friendly, or people won't like you." Both of them sometimes found themselves pretending they liked people, places, and activities they really didn't like, making gestures of generosity and friendliness they didn't really mean.

Psychologically, it is probably not possible that Debbie's mother's single reprimand was traumatizing enough by itself to have a lifelong effect. More probably, that single experience verbalized an assumption that was already felt within Debbie and her mother. That the incident was remembered by both of them is evidence that it had clearly articulated an old, familiar part of their belief system: "If you aren't friendly, you aren't lovable."

Most children are attracted to friendly pets and genuinely friendly people. Though children probably don't reflect on it, they are aware of the attractive power of friendliness. Adults generally have a similar experience. Being friendly is associated with relating in a loving context, an important cornerstone in developing healthy self-esteem. To be labeled as unfriendly is to be vulnerable to isolation and excluded from those relationships that sustain life, strengthen one's sense of self, and foster meaningfulness.

2. Disliked

Although the label "disliked" ranked second among the total sample, it ranked first among the males. (See Figure 14.)

Fear of being disliked had its highest weight among the

Figure 14
COMPARISON OF RELATING LABELS RANKED BETWEEN FEMALES AND MALES

Rank	Females (N=231)	Weighted Score	Males (N=198)	Weighted Score
1	Unfriendly	123	Disliked	118
2	Disliked	102	Unfriendly	111
3	Ungrateful	65	Ungrateful	52
4	Unattractive	45	Unattractive	52
5	Impolite	41	Impolite	51
6	Jealous	24	Jealous	16

high school boys in our sample and remained strong for males throughout the young adult years. After forty, the fear appeared to lose some of its force, though not much.

Certain common questions tend to surface when I am labeled "disliked," for example: What must I do to become liked? What will transform me into a likable person? What price must I pay? How much of my own likes must I forego to be liked?

The fear of being disliked or unlikable triggers primitive fears in us of not being wanted, not being invited to belong. If this fear has been operating since childhood, it may stir up childhood fears of abandonment. From the child's perspective, to be abandoned by the mother or the family is to be left to die, since the child is helpless when unprotected and left to face the elements alone.

The teenage fear of social abandonment reflects the childhood fear of physical abandonment. Since neither family nor social group is obliged to accept me, I must be likable in order to be wanted. Yet who can clearly say what it is that makes a person liked or disliked?

For example, in high school, Ken feared being disliked. Whenever the other boys asked him to go out, he would go with them even when he didn't feel like it, for fear they would say they didn't like him. He told us of an incident.

> Tim called me one night with the usual "Let's go out and do something." I couldn't honestly tell him I was too busy, and I didn't dare say I didn't want to go out, for fear he wouldn't like me. So I said okay. Actually, I had a cold, and my favorite Christmas story was on television, *How the Grinch Stole Christmas*. I just wanted to curl up with my dog and have a quiet evening at home. It was also one of the few times my dad was at home and not very busy, and we were having a good time together.

But Ken went out with the boys anyway, aggravating the bad cold, missing his favorite story, and displeasing his father, who had been enjoying the evening together as much as Ken. All this happened because Ken was afraid someone might dislike him. Fear of what the neighbors might say deprived Ken of time at home that he wanted and probably really needed.

3. Ungrateful

The label "ungrateful" evoked the third-highest amount of worry and fear among our sample of men and women. Being called ungrateful seems to be of special concern to young adult women, twice as much so as the corresponding group of men. Perhaps one reason for this emphasis in young women is that, since many of them are mothers, they want to impress their children with the need to be grateful. Also, to many young adult women falls the task of building friendly bonds among their new neighbors, and they feel that gratitude helps build a neighborly spirit.

One expression of gratitude very common in the United States is the thank-you note or the thank-you phone call. Parents who want their children to be seen as grateful frequently pressure them to write thank-you notes for gifts received, often to the point of inauthenticity. For example, a child who had hoped for a toy may be required to find a new way of thanking grandmother for unwanted handkerchiefs the third year in a row.

People who are particularly concerned about being labeled ungrateful may feel they must return favors by outdoing the favors done to them. We talked to a young adult, single woman who was preoccupied with being seen as grateful. When invited by a family to dinner, she often takes separate gifts for each family member, even when she knows a general gift to be enjoyed by everyone, such as flowers or a box of candy, would satisfy even the strictest sense of etiquette. But something special goes on in this young woman's mind.

> The necessity of bringing all those gifts is not realistic when I think about it, but somewhere deep inside me there is a little voice that says, "You don't deserve to be treated as a valuable person, so you better pay for any kindness you receive from others." As I look at it now, it seems I'm trying to buy someone's valuing of me. Though when I do it, I tell myself I don't want to be seen as ungrateful.

The inner impulse to pay for what is given often blinds people from seeing their friends' love as the free gift it is because they cannot see themselves as lovable and valuable.

One characteristic of persons preoccupied with gratitude is the habit of overthanking. One man said, "I can think of a thousand times I've overthanked people for things. I guess I just wanted to make sure that I was seen as grateful, and not as ungrateful."

People concerned about what the neighbors might say usually also wish to be seen as "nice" people. This wish leads people to being very self-critical in an effort to control their behavior so that they come across as "nice" beyond question. Since persons can never fully live up to that inner ideal, they soon become overwhelmed.

Meg is a young wife and mother often overwhelmed by the fear of being labeled ungrateful.

> In order to show that I am truly grateful for Christmas presents given to our family, I feel I have to show that each gift was specially chosen. I have to make the giver feel personally good—no matter what the gift. I realize this is a hard task and makes great demands on my creativity. I want each note to be unique, almost as if people were going to compare them. Because the task seems overwhelming, I put it off till

> it seems long overdue. Then I wonder how I'm going to explain that I'm really a grateful person if I've let so much time go by without expressing my gratitude. At that point, I wish I could just chuck the whole business of writing thank-you notes.

It seems that to be seen as ungrateful is to be seen as socially inept and, therefore, not socially desirable. At bottom, the fear of being called ungrateful probably has to do with the fear of social exclusion and the loss of that sense of security based on belongingness.

4. Unattractive

Both men and woman rank "unattractive" fourth as a label they fear being applied to them. The highest anxiety over this label is shown by high school girls, two out of three marking "unattractive" as a first, second, or third concern. From college age on, women's concern over this label drops continuously till in the over-forty group not even one in thirty women bothers to mark it.

Among the male sample, the highest focus on attractiveness seems to occur during high school and again among the young adults.

The need to be seen as attractive for the youngest group seems to be related to popularity. Attractiveness is seen as a gateway to some of the good things in life. Being attractive can help you get good friends, a good spouse, and even a good job. Perhaps, after forty, the need to be attractive is no longer as important to people as their experience and competence.

One high school girl refused to go to parties because she felt plump and unattractive, and consequently very vulnerable to her peers.

Two teenage sisters would walk from their apartment to the swimming pool with towels wrapped around their entire bodies because they saw themselves as fat and unattractive. They dropped the towels only a moment before they plunged into the pool so that no one would have to look at their slightly overweight bodies. Their fear was that the neighbors would say, "How fat and unattractive!" To us, they seemed like two vital teenagers, who might be a few pounds overweight but in no way physically unattractive.

Typically, adolescents are preoccupied with their bodies, with a tendency to be supercritical and hyperjudgmental about their physical features. It is also natural for adolescents to criticize one another, which only tends to reflect their sensitivity about any lack of perfection in themselves. Their envy of physically attractive classmates only heightens the discomfort they feel about how their own bodies appear to others.

Makeup has been commercialized as necessary to attractiveness in women. Several wives told of getting up earlier than their husbands, and getting fully dressed with makeup on to look as attractive as possible at breakfast.

Two adolescents, a boy and a girl, told us how their mother often avoided being touched because she felt her hair and makeup must be kept perfect. It was as if once she lost her perfectly groomed look she became insecure and felt unattractive.

An angry college-age daughter came to complain about her father, who had embarrassed her by being very unkempt and crude when her date arrived to pick her up. She felt her father's unattractiveness affected her attractiveness and turned off potential boyfriends. "Dad cared a lot about what *his* friends said, but he didn't give a damn about the impression he made on *my* friends."

This young woman underlines the fact that many people feel affected by labeling applied to their family or heritage.

5. Impolite

The labels "impolite" and "ungrateful" run close together in importance. The two labels may be related since a lack of gratitude is often mentioned as a sign of impoliteness.

Figure 15
COMPARISON OF "IMPOLITE" LABEL CONCERN
BETWEEN MALES AND FEMALES
(weighted scores given)

Category	High School	College Age	Young Adults	Over Forty	Total
Females	7	14	11	9	41
Males	7	12	11	21	51

Among women in our sample, the college group shows most concern over impoliteness. This concern declines for older females.

Surprisingly, the males over forty show a significant jump in concern about being labeled impolite; it is almost twice as high as the score of the younger men, and more than both groups of women past college age combined.

Impolite is a generic term whose meaning could include being ungrateful, thoughtless, forgetful of etiquette, rude, ungracious, unattentive, and a host of other negative terms. Besides, the label is ambiguous. For example, there are times when it seems more polite to listen than to talk, while at other times the reverse is true.

Pam was at a dinner party with some people she'd never met, but they were people important to her fiancé. Pam wanted them to like her, but it happened to be a time when she was distracted with many other problems and didn't feel like talking. She was able to be quiet, friendly, a good listener, and even helpful to the hostess getting the meal on and off the table. But for her that wasn't enough. She felt she would be impolite if she wasn't entertaining, vivacious, talkative.

"I couldn't see that what I brought to the party was enough," she explained. "Since I wasn't at my best, I assumed only my best was good enough. I also assumed others would want more from me and if I didn't give it I was being impolite."

The point here is that fear of being impolite crippled Pam's ability to enjoy herself and to let others enjoy her. If she had not been preoccupied with being seen as impolite, she could have realized that people seeing her for the first time would be content with whatever of herself she brought. Though they might have learned more about her if she had talked more about herself, they did meet a genuine part of her, the quiet listener who was happy to hear about other people's lives.

By being caught up in a fear of being labeled impolite, or caught up in an obligation to do the polite thing, people do themselves out of the joy of just being with each other. Such fears effectively block spontaneity and the obvious delights of being with loving people.

6. Jealous

Although "jealous" is the label that aroused least concern among our sample, it reached its maximum amount of impact as a fear among men over forty.

Women over forty, by the way, are twice as concerned about being labeled jealous (6 percent) as they are unattractive (3 percent).

A woman told us about her father, who was jealous but couldn't tolerate being told so. He worked a regular eight-hour day and often went hunting or fishing with friends after work, so he was out of the house most of the time. But whenever he was at home, he wanted his wife to be there for him. If she went out visiting some of her friends or was called on the phone while he was at home, he was apparently very jealous of her attention to anyone else. Their daughter told us the following story.

> I can remember dad sending me across the street to get my mother. "Tell her she has a phone call," my father ordered. I relayed the message and my mother dutifully came home, except there wasn't any phone call. My father scowled when she came in. She asked, "Why did you send Nora to tell me there was a phone call when there wasn't one?" My father just kept scowling. Finally he said, "You spend too much time across the street."

Nora's father was also jealous of the time her mother spent with the children. Her father's jealousy and authoritarian style never got challenged. "I guess I grew up thinking my father had the right to be jealous and bossy," Nora explained. "However, my mother certainly didn't have the same right. I've always been afraid of being seen as jealous and confused about my rights in a relationship."

Fear of being seen as jealous may well keep Nora out of touch with her own healthy instincts and rights. We found many of the college population, like Nora, more concerned with how they would be seen, e.g., as jealous, than with their own feelings and rights.

At a women's college we discovered among students much gossiping and flirting with each other's boyfriends. Again and again we heard them say they didn't want others to think of them as jealous, even when they minded one of their friends friend or boyfriend to think they were upset or that their rights were being ignored. On the other side of the coin, the flirtatious friends were equally afraid of making someone jealous. In general, because of this fear, relationships at the college were filled with confused feelings and mixed communications.

During late adolescence, when popularity and ego-development are intensely felt drives, issues get very confused. It is a time for testing one's powers but not overstepping the rules for belonging to the group. The wish to be seen as popular and desirable conflict with one's fears of being judged as seductive or jealous.

Write-in Labels

In addition to the six relating labels suggested in the questionnaire, our respondents produced a large number of write-ins. Among the women, other unwelcome relating labels mentioned more than once included snobbish, bitchy, conceited, selfish, rude, boring, pushy, unpopular, cynical, and sexually loose. Other unwelcome relating labels mentioned by men or women more than once included conceited, insensitive, selfish, prudish, and alcoholic. Though these write-in labels have little relevance statistically, they are obviously important for the individuals who took the time to write them on the questionnaire. It also suggests that unwelcome relating labels elicit a broad concern in people.

CHAPTER 8

Competence Labels People Fear

Since people in contemporary society are recognized more for what they do than for what they feel, it is not surprising they would be concerned about what the neighbors are saying about their ability to be effective and productive.

Formal competency evaluations are announced continuously during school years by test scores, grades, and report cards. Informal comments regarding our competency begin long before school and continue long after a diploma is received. We fear being called stupid or a failure. We hope people will think of us as good parents or good workers, yet we worry that others will notice our mistakes and label us "bad." At work or at home, we long to be recognized as responsible, well organized, and successful. Secretly, we are afraid people will see us as just the opposite.

In our survey of competency fears, we asked respondents to rank six labels: stupid, a failure, disorganized, incompetent, irresponsible, and a "bad" parent, child, friend, or worker. We wanted to find out which labels evoked the most fearful responses in them. We weighted heaviest the label they ranked as their first fear (three points), less heavy the label they ranked second (two points), and least heavy the label they ranked third (one point). Figure 16 presents a summary of responses concerning the six competency labels.

Clearly, the general label "incompetent" evoked most con-

Figure 16
SUMMARY RANKING OF COMPETENCY LABELS
(total sample N=429)

Rank	Labels	Weighted Score
1	Incompetent	190
2	Irresponsible	168
3	A Failure	149
4	Stupid	134
5	A Bad . . . Parent, Child, Friend, Worker, etc.	99
6	Disorganized	67

cern among our sample, with "irresponsible" taking a close second place, especially for female respondents. (See Table A-4 in the Appendix.)

In the following sections of this chapter, we examine the meaning and intent of all six labels, since each of these labels will have different significance for people at different ages.

Discussing competency, we noticed a general trend in people to take an either/or attitude with regard to the labels, saying for example, "I'm either smart or stupid, I'm either a success or a failure, I'm either a good parent or a bad one." The sense they communicate is, if they're not smart, they must be stupid. If they don't feel totally good, then they're bad. An attitude powerfully ingrained among many people is that anything less than perfect is imperfect, and therefore undesirable and unacceptable.

We noticed another common phenomenon regarding competency. Many people internalize neighbors' comments about their stupidity, irresponsibility, and competency. Then, even when outer neighbors are no longer assigning a pejorative label to them, an inner neighbor's voice is still doing so. The process turned inward becomes insidiously damaging to the personality.

1. Incompetent

In the area of competency, the general label "incompetent" is the one most feared by both the men and women in our sample. Its growth over time as a concern over what the neighbors will say has some interesting changes. Among our male respondents, this label continued to grow steadily in importance from high school through college and onward through the adult years. In contrast, among the female sample, concern over being called incompetent reached its peak (thirty-three weighted score) among the young adult sample, the time of career and family building; and then among the over-forty group, scores dropped back to college-age levels.

Figure 17
COMPARISON OF "INCOMPETENT" LABEL BETWEEN FEMALES AND MALES
(weighted scored given)

Category	High School	College Age	Young Adults	Over Forty	Total
Females (N = 231)	11	22	33	22	88
Males (N = 198)	22	23	26	31	102

"What does it mean to be called incompetent?" we asked our respondents. Here are some of their replies: "I'm clumsy." "I'm a klutz." "I can't do it right." "I lack training." "I have no skill." "I'm unsuited." "I'm unfit and unable." "I'm deficient." "I'm unprofessional." "I'm untalented." "I'm unskilled." "I'm discredited and disqualified." "I'm wrong."

A certain finality is implied in calling someone incompetent, which makes the label especially fearful. One woman said, "What's missing when I hear the word *incompetent* is a quality of hope. Incompetency is presented as a static state; it implies you're dealing with a permanently damaged person." A man echoed her sentiments. "The invitation to become competent is not implied in calling someone incompetent; it's like a degenerative process."

Perhaps the label generates strong fears, not only because it is vague and general, but also because, in the eyes of most people, to be named incompetent is a final judgment. Incompetent nurses or doctors are not to be trusted since they are deemed dangerous and potentially destructive.

In the job market, only competent people need apply. One who merits the epithet incompetent becomes unwanted, unhelpful, incapable, a burden, and even a threat.

A sense of incompetency often is felt first in childhood. In order to receive acknowledgment from parents, or to avoid their criticism and punishment, a child gets the sense he or she should be *better*. However, some parents expect their children to do things better, but do not give the children adequate feedback to know when they have done something well enough. Without helpful feedback, such children lack a measuring device to know when they are doing well enough. The absence of supportive parental feedback generates children who keep hoping, "If I try harder and do it a little better, maybe I'll get the praise I want." Intuitively, they know they need parental acknowledgment and affirmation. Yet unless they are clearly told they are acting competently for their age, they keep trying harder, always pushing to do things better, but never able to let go of the now internalized and feared label "incompetent," or one of its many variations.

As such children grow older, they often become adults who cannot "hear" when people affirm their competence. Their fear that people will say "It's not good enough" is so strong that this is what they "hear," even when people clearly offer approval and praise. Their sense of incompetency is so internalized that their competency cannot be acknowledged. Paradoxically, the label "incompetent," which they fear to hear, they manage always to hear, even when it isn't spoken.

For example, Nancy, a highly sought-after nurse, does not recognize her own competence. She doesn't believe it of herself, despite all her years of nursing work and accomplishment. She seems to forget or deny any of her competence. "All during nurses' training," she explained, "I felt I wasn't doing well enough. I would say to myself, 'If only you had spent more time preparing, you could have done better.' If I didn't get an A on an exam, I would feel incompetent. Even when I did get an A, I knew my exam wasn't perfect."

When we met her, Nancy had been a teacher of nurses for a number of years. Again she kept talking about doing it better, echoing inside herself both the inner neighbor who labeled her incompetent and the child still hoping to receive the desired affirmation she never received from her parents. When asked what the student nurses thought about her as a teacher, she replied, "They said I was the best teacher they ever had." In Nancy's case, the student-nurse neighbors are speaking and directly affirming her, but some inner voice argues otherwise, prohibiting her from acknowledging her competence.

There is a saying, which seems to be echoed by many of the Christian churches, that goes like this: "Something can be done well only if it requires much effort and pain." Nancy echoed this sentiment the time she organized a social event for her church. When the pastor told her what a good job she'd done, Nancy couldn't acknowledge her competency because it hadn't taken very much of her time and energy, and it wasn't painful. The fear of incompetence, or of just not doing things as well as they could be done, is a tremendous burden in Nancy's life. It robs her of much joy, sense of accomplishment, and self-esteem. At a deep level, it robs her of her inner peace and security.

2. Irresponsible

"Irresponsible," second in importance among competency labels for both men and women in our sample, is particularly high among the concerns of high school girls and ranks highest in this category for women over forty. Evidently these are periods of life when the "irresponsible" label seems most devastating.

As with many of the competency labels, when people fear being labeled, for example, "irresponsible," they often bend over backward to appear responsible and to feel responsible even for matters out of their control.

When we asked one woman, who marked irresponsible as her primary fear, how she felt about her responsibilities, a long list of them tumbled out of her mouth.

> I feel irresponsible in my neighborhood when I don't keep my grass cut and my leaves raked. I feel irresponsible when the dog gets out of the yard, I feel irresponsible when the snow on our sidewalk is not shoveled. It's not that I worry that people might slip and fall. The first thought I have is that people would think of me as irresponsible, not doing my part in keeping the neighborhood up. If a neighbor complained about my children's music playing too loudly, I'd feel I should have been more responsible and noticed the noise before my neighbor pointed it out. I feel that if my children or my dogs are disturbing the neighbors it's a reflection of me and my lack of responsibility.

Another mother's sense of irresponsibility revolved around her daughter. "If my daughter has an opportunity to participate in something like a school play or a class dance and I resist finding the time in my own schedule to make the necessary chauffeuring trips, I feel somehow irresponsible in my duties as a parent. It's as though I'm keeping her from her fullest potential." This mother feels overwhelmed by her own perspective on responsibility since her daughter is multitalented and involved in ballet, art, voice, guitar, and drama. "Because Kim is interested in all these things and interested in developing them in herself, I feel that a really responsible parent would encourage and facilitate all of it, and would be selfish and irresponsible to resist."

Many who fear the "irresponsible" label see themselves as abandoners.

Freshmen college students often turn up in the counseling center at the beginning of the school year out of concern for their parents' welfare. Some are afraid that while they are away from home their parents will drink too much or fight too much and maybe even get divorced. Such students talk as if they were responsible for their parents and by coming to college had somehow abandoned them.

One student named Judy vividly remembered a lady in the grocery store at home who said, "I don't know what your mother will do without you when you go off to college." Judy didn't hear the lady's comment as a compliment, which is probably how she meant it, but as a warning that when she went off to college it would be a burdensome time for her mother. The weight of responsibility Judy had assumed was painful to her. She acknowledged it was not exactly irresponsible for her to go to college, but "almost," she said. It is not uncommon for parents to separate after the youngest child goes off to college, and Judy's parents were one of those couples who did separate. When they did, her inner voice accused her of irresponsibility. "If I had stayed at home, the problems between my parents would not have come to a head. I could have been the connection that kept them together. I shouldn't have gone away to college."

Among overly responsible students, having fun is often taken as a sign of irresponsibility. To make even a small amount of fun acceptable, they feel the need to become extremely conscientious students. Paying a high price for their new freedom from family responsibility, they show their responsibility to family now by getting very high grades. Fran was one student who had a difficult time accepting anything less than an A, for to her it would be a sign she was not fully responsible. Any lower grade would signal a self-accusation that she was not studying hard enough. It felt to her as though her family were right there at college with her, evaluating her every move, checking out how responsible she was. Under this inner voiced scrutiny, she drove herself relentlessly.

Inner direction and a sense of responsibility are very important in life. However, they need to be experienced with a healthy sense of reality, provided by a balanced perspective on all the circumstances, and an appreciation for joy and the complexity of life.

3. Failure

Being labeled a failure received the highest amount of concern among high school girls. For them, this label ranked even higher than "irresponsible" and "incompetent." More than three out of every four girls in our high school sample marked being called a failure as their first, second, or third concern. High school boys also ranked this label highest in this category. Two out of every three boys in our sample marked "a failure" as one of their fears.

Figure 18
RANKED COMPARISON OF COMPETENCY LABELS BETWEEN HIGH SCHOOL BOYS AND GIRLS

Rank	High School Girls (N=48)	Weighted Score	High School Boys (N=46)	Weighted Score
1	A Failure	28	A Failure	25
2	Irresponsible	25	Irresponsible	22
3	Stupid	19	Incompetent	22
4	A Bad . . . Parent, Child, Friend, Worker, etc.	14	Stupid	18
5	Incompetent	11	A Bad . . . Parent, Child, Friend, Worker, etc.	11
6	Disorganized	4	Disorganized	2

As a label, being a failure seems to lose its force as people grow older; in the over-forty group, this label drops to less than half the concern it elicited in high school. (See Table A-4 in the Appendix.)

What are some of the ways people describe being a failure? A washout, a loser, a dropout, a flunker, a real zero, unsellable, bankrupt, unsuccessful, a reject, someone who didn't try hard enough.

Like many of the labels in the competency area, failure is often bestowed at an early age. Remembering early failures, even for older people, is very easy, since failures tend to be powerfully registered experiences.

A high school girl vividly remembered failing a spelling test in the second grade. It was the only time she ever failed, but the embarrassment of it made an indelible mark on her memory. She was supposed to take her test paper home and show it to her parents, but she threw it in the wastebasket as soon as she got home. When asked what her parents might have done had she shown them the spelling paper, she said she didn't have any fantasies of being scolded, punished, or otherwise negatively reacted to by them. Rather, it was already her own inner reaction she could not tolerate. She did not want anyone to see her shame at failing.

A very devout nurse with a perfectionist bent was invited to pray over a boy suffering from cancer. The compassionate part of her wanted to do it. "But if I tried it and the boy didn't heal," she explained, "I would see myself as a failure." Furthermore, she wouldn't let herself try it because if she went to his room (and failed) she felt she would have been presenting herself as someone able to heal by prayer. What she forgot was that the request had simply been to "come and pray"; her fears relating to the issue of failure had translated the request to pray into a request to heal the child's cancer.

Fear of failure is expressed by the aging scientist who fears he will not be able to maintain his memory ability and keep up his research productivity; the woman who fears her husband's new boss will not like the dinner she's prepared and they will fail to make a good impression on him; the people who fear they will fail to keep up-to-date—financially, politically, informationally, and so on.

What makes some people respond to a challenge with the fearful comment "I'll probably fail"? Those who have this fear also admit they have a lot more fear of failure than experience of it.

Feeling sure she'd fail, Penny was afraid to take the social worker–licensing exam, even though she had no basis for her fear. One day, she brought home a brochure about the exam, which contained half a dozen sample questions. Her husband, trying to help her be realistic about the exam, read the first question aloud to her. Penny immediately panicked. "See, I don't know the answer. I'd fail." Instead of going along with her panic and sense of failure, her husband calmly suggested, "Let's let the first question go for now and see how you do with the second one." Penny answered the second question easily, as she did the third, fourth, fifth, and sixth. Then her husband asked the first question again. This time she answered it confidently. In that confident spirit she signed up for the licensing test and passed it. Penny was the same woman who for years had maintained she would fail that test.

We asked a middle-aged woman who had for most of her life been fearful of failure how she got that way.

"I'm not sure this is all of it by any means," she began, "but I remember being told in Sunday school that we were all created with the potential to be perfect. We were told we should strive to be perfect, for we needed to be perfect to get to heaven. And since we were told about many saints who made it to heaven, obviously it was possible, if I just tried hard enough. As a child I wanted to be good, I wanted to go to heaven and have my parents proud of me. That's probably a part of my fear of failure: having to deal with the idea that people I love might be ashamed of me." Even now as an adult, though this woman knows intellectually that to be perfect is an impossibility and an unrealistic expectation, her gut feeling and fear of failure remains a powerful influence in her daily life and often cripples her from meeting challenges with confidence and full functionality.

4. Stupid

While "failure" is a label that may be broadly applied, stupid is usually reserved to describe a lack of intelligence. It is a label that remains strongly feared by women throughout life, though in our sample worry about being called stupid reached its peak among women in college. Well over half these women marked "stupid" as one of their fears. At every age level, female fear of the label is higher than that of men in the sample.

Figure 19
COMPARISON OF "STUPID" LABEL
BETWEEN FEMALES AND MALES
(weighted scores given)

Category	High School	College Age	Young Adults	Over Forty	Total
Females	19	21	17	15	72
Males	18	16	15	13	62

What do people hear in their minds when they are called stupid? Some of their responses include synonyms like dumb, ignorant, unintelligent, foolish, witless, empty-headed, feeble-minded, easily confused, and not bright, smart, or clever, or expressions such as half-wit, idiot, moron, imbecile, oaf, fuzzy thinker, poor learner, and slow learner.

"Stupid" is a label feared most in academic settings, especially but paradoxically among people who are least likely to be so named.

About forty new doctoral candidates, representing a variety of disciplines, gathered at Saint Petersburg, Florida, to spend a month together exchanging information, impacting on each other, and forming a multidisciplined community of learners. For that month, they were expected to be an interacting community, a band of curious and observant neighbors.

"As I looked around at my new graduate-school neighbors," said Marion, "I felt sure everyone of them was brilliant, except me."

During an introductory meeting at which the new doctoral students introduced themselves, spelling out their accomplishments and goals, Marion was left feeling in awe of everyone, confirming her worst fears of feeling stupid.

After several days her anxiety reached overwhelming proportions, so she decided to admit to the group how stupid and inadequate she felt. When she did, a marvelous and surprising thing happened. There was a sudden surge of recognition in the group, a break in tension, and then bursts of laughter. "One by one," said Marion, "we made the discovery that each of us shared much the same fantasy and fear—that of being found out as 'not very bright' by the others." As the group laughed and compared versions of their fear of being seen as stupid, Marion went on to explain, they breathed a sigh of relief that the bogeyman had been unmasked. They found not only were they in no real danger from each other, but there was a friendly commonality to be shared.

This fear of being called stupid also has an effect in nonacademic settings. People who report a fear of being called stupid often find this fear hovers over them in groups, especially where they may be newcomers.

"This fear often plagues me," reported an executive's wife. "I have a tendency to listen very critically to everything I hear *me* saying. Then I obsess over everything I have said. Because of this, when others in the group are talking I usually wind up not listening very closely." She further explained how her obsession with being seen as stupid could cripple her ability to speak. "During conversations, again and again in my mind I keep rephrasing and refining my reply to make it 'just right'—an impossible task! I often give up trying to formulate the perfect reply; or else the proper moment for my contribution passes by. So in the end I either appear slightly awkward making my belated reply or I don't make it at all. Either way I feel stupid and afraid other people in the group are thinking of me as a stupid person."

One thing this young woman might begin doing is trusting that her original, spontaneously formulated reply would be "good enough" and trust the group members to be open and generous in their reaction to her. In this way, her change in attitude would lead to a change in behavior, which would likely lead to a healthy change in self-concept.

5. A Bad . . . Parent, Child, Friend, Worker, etc.

Almost twice as much weighted concern was given to the "bad" label by women than by men. Women seemed much more susceptible than men to being called a bad parent, child, friend, worker, etc. Women over forty seemed especially concerned about being labeled a "bad" something or other. The emphasis of the fear in this label is on "bad." It is felt in contrast to the "good" little girls and boys children were told to be.

"Bad" is a very amorphous label, one very difficult to defend against. As a judgment of competence, it lacks any measure or proportion. After all, how bad is bad?

What range of meaning does "bad" have for people? When we asked about the meaning of a *bad child*, we received replies like delinquent, spoiled, impolite, unclean, misbehaved, ungrateful, unhelpful, disrespectful, disobedient, undisciplined, and so on.

When we asked about *bad parents*, we received descriptions that included worthless, abusive, wicked, harmful, uninterested, punishing, impatient, and neglectful.

Bad spouses were seen as immoral, unfaithful, uncommitted, thoughtless, offensive, disagreeable, jealous, cruel, cheating, uncaring, and immature.

Bad friends were labeled as forgetful, picky, disloyal, dishonest, mean, insensitive, unpleasant, self-centered, vulgar, and disagreeable.

The ambiguity of the "bad" label helped to make it more fearful. For example, we found parents, who were afraid of being labeled "bad" by their neighbors, asking us about it. "Who is a bad parent?" one father asked. "If I quit beating my child, do I become a good parent? Is someone a bad parent who works two jobs to financially survive, but is seldom home to play with the children?"

A mother asked, "But how bad am I? My adolescent daughters tell me I should sit down and listen to their problems. My ten-year-old son wants me to attend all his Little League games. If I were a good parent, they tell me, I'd do these things. So I must be a bad one. Yet I read about parents who neglect and batter their children and could be indicted for child abuse. Am I in the same category of badness as they are?"

When the "bad" label is applied to you, it is important first of all to ask who it is who is calling you, for example, a bad parent. Is it your next-door neighbor who hears you losing your temper with your children? Is it the unknown shopper who sees you slap your child impatiently in a grocery store? Is it the teachers in school who feel you don't show enough interest in your child's academic progress? Is it your own parents who say you don't discipline your children, you spoil them, you're never home with them, or you don't feed them proper food? Or is it your own children who imply you're a bad parent when you won't conform to their wishes or expectations?

A single, working woman was dismayed that people would consider her a bad friend because she did not put enough "energy" into her relationships. "I don't fear being considered a bad friend out of disloyalty," she explained. "I'm not at all disloyal to my friends. I don't betray them or the secrets they tell me. My weak point is follow-through. I like my friends a lot, but I never seem to make enough room in my life for them. I don't take the initiative to get together and do things together. Often I don't bother to answer letters or phone calls. When they tell me I'm never *available,* that's the word that makes me think I'm a bad friend."

Other neighbors to which many people are vulnerable are parents. From childhood, parents' negative evaluations are so internalized that even at times when mom and dad aren't telling you you're a bad person, you hear the condemnation echoing inside you just the same.

"Can I disappoint someone I love and still not be seen as bad?" asked one young man who went on to answer himself, "In my head I hear yes, but in my emotions I hear a lot of static. Maybe I need to clear the channel."

6. Disorganized

Although being disorganized seems to describe most of the human race, it was the label least feared by our sample. Perhaps because it is such a common quality, and because many people freely admit being disorganized, the label seems to generate little worry. It does not command the fearful attention of more overwhelming labels such as "incompetent," "irresponsible," and "a failure."

Very few high school students of either sex seem concerned about this label, and although it did evoke reaction from a small set of older women, those that were affected most strongly by being labeled "disorganized" were the adult men. Perhaps among women "disorganized" is not a very threatening label, while for men who are culturally expected to be rational, clearheaded, and well organized, the label may be somewhat more embarrassing and ego-deflating.

What does it mean to people to be called disorganized? Here are some of their expressions: confused, cluttered, disorderly, irrational, unstructured, undisciplined, mixed up, diffuse, unfocused, unsystematized, unmethodical, disturbed, disoriented, illogical, turbulent, and spacey.

People concerned with being labeled disorganized offer typical comments that are repeated again and again. For example, "Every time someone comes into my office and sees my cluttered desk I'm sure they're saying, 'How disorganized!' But I know exactly where everything is on that desk."

Or another version: "When I'm trying to live out my many roles at one time—parent, friend, career person—and going off in four or five directions, instead of presuming people would appreciate how well I handle a number of busy roles, I would be more apt to imagine them saying I'm disorganized."

Or a third: "When I visit people whose homes or offices are neatly kept, I tend to evaluate them as much more organized than I am. If I'm particularly down on myself at the time, I'll probably reprimand myself for being so disorganized."

People often project their own critical self-judgments onto others, then feel defensive and vulnerable. At such times it is well to remember that neighborly concern is usually mutual, that is, if I am concerned over what my neighbor might say about me, I can presume my neighbor is concerned about what I say about him or her. In the neighborly dynamic, we have two people who respect and want the respect of each other. Both are typically vulnerable to criticism, both presuming their own flaws are clearly noticeable to the other. This is the common pattern.

It is our hope that understanding neighborly patterns will mitigate some of the fears and help facilitate the kind of caring and support that calls forth greater wholeness and freedom in relationship.

CHAPTER 9

Inner Quality Labels People Fear

In our questionnaire, the third set of labels we studied were called *inner qualities.* We called these eight labels—cruel, stingy, superficial, lazy, immoral, boastful, self-centered, and phony—inner qualities because persons usually associate the positive sides of them with values and attitudes that are essential elements of the self. To attack or deny these positive inner qualities is to threaten one's personal core. Everyone would rather be seen as kind rather than cruel, generous rather than stingy, deep and perceptive rather than shallow and superficial, industrious rather than lazy, ethically responsible rather than immoral, modest rather than boastful, concerned about others rather than self-centered, and genuine rather than phony.

In our survey of concern over negative inner-quality labels, we asked people to give first, second, and third rank to the eight labels. We weighted their first choice highest (three points), their second next highest (two points), and their third least highest (one point).

Figure 20 presents a summary of ranking for inner-quality labels for the total group.

Although self-centeredness and being phony are clearly the variables evoking most concern in general, the other six labels offer interesting insights into the dynamic workings of the fear

Figure 20
SUMMARY RANKING OF
INNER-QUALITY LABELS FEARED
(total sample N = 429)

Rank	Label	Weighted Score
1	Self-centered	174
2	Phony	171
3	Cruel	119
4	Superficial	98
5	Lazy	70
6	Immoral	63
7	Stingy	49
8	Boastful	48

of what neighbors might say. Thus, we consider each of the eight labels in turn according to their rank.

Some of the write-in inner qualities that respondents to our questionnaire feared being labeled included: thoughtless, cold, unfeeling, uncaring, insincere, dishonest, untrustworthy, conceited, stubborn, boring, judgmental, manipulative, self-pitying, wishy-washy, sexually inadequate, and alcoholic. None of these labels were mentioned more than twice in our entire sample, so they have no statistical relevance, though for the individuals who took the time to write them in they certainly were personally important. They do reinforce the hypothesis that people are anxious about what their neighbors say about them, and that certain labels evoke stronger responses than others.

1. Self-Centered

Across our total sample, "self-centered" was the negative inner-quality label people most worried about.

For women in general, it was clearly the most unwelcome label, showing its highest concern among high school girls (four out of five gave it a rank), and remaining first for women in college, as well as for the young adult group.

Figure 21
COMPARISON OF RESPONSES TO "SELF-CENTERED" LABEL BETWEEN FEMALES AND MALES
(weighted scores given)

Category	High School	College Age	Young Adults	Over Forty	Total
Females	33	23	22	19	97
Males	26	18	21	12	77

For men in general, "self-centered" ranked second in importance, but for high school boys it was far and away the most important inner-quality label they feared.

After forty, concern for the label drops off significantly for men, less so for women.

What does it mean to people when they hear the word *self-centered*? What other words strike them as similar? According to people we talked to, self-centered generates expressions such as narcissistic, egocentric, selfish, egotistic, conceited, stuck-up, stuck on yourself, center of the stage, self-admiring, self-applauding, a big ego, center of the world, interested in no one else, unconcerned about others, a spoiled brat, and so on.

Michele is a teenager trying to sort out how attractive she is, but she's stuck with the label self-centered and feels her two older sisters gave it to her. She described how she used to enjoy spending time with them, talking about how she would like to do her hair, or whether she should lose weight. But once she overheard her sisters call her self-centered. They said, "Michele is always acting as though she's being watched and admired." She remains concerned about her attractiveness and self-conscious about how she looks, but now she spends time looking at herself in the mirror, trying on different clothes, and posing, *when her sisters aren't around.* Since she overheard her sisters, she's become very sensitive about comments they might make. She fears being called self-centered, yet is stuck with thinking of herself as self-centered. More accurately, she is a young girl struggling with a lack of self-esteem, and confused as to how desirable and acceptable she is in her own eyes as well as the eyes of others.

Marilyn, a social worker who just turned thirty years old, described herself to us as being self-centered. "I seem to be always talking about myself," she said. "Even I get sick of hearing myself talk sometimes!" She fears that coming to therapy sessions for herself only encourages her narcissism. "I'd be better off making myself very busy instead of coming here to think about myself and talk about myself." She's afraid of appearing self-centered in groups. "I often stay very quiet at parties because I'm afraid I'll just start talking about myself and I'll be seen as self-centered. But then I'm afraid that my quietness will be taken as aloofness or a lack of interest and people will think I'm not very friendly or entertaining." Marilyn's fear of what the neighbors might say can eventually cripple her emotionally. "I'm at the point now where I often dread going out socially," she admitted.

Claire often refused dinner invitations for her and her husband without telling him because she felt he was so self-centered he would cause them as a couple to be rejected by their acquaintances. "Better to refuse an invitation than be disliked and rejected," she concluded.

What are the common traits in people that tend to evoke the "self-centered" label? The most common ones are selfishness, being uncooperative, and lacking consideration of others. Elli scored high on all three counts. She incessantly talked about her life, her feelings, her plans, her fears, her accomplishments, yet never thought to ask how things were going with others. She never hesitated to ask for favors and was surprised when anyone said no to her; yet when people asked her to do a favor for them, she would reply, "I'll see if it fits in with my plans." Usually it didn't. If someone began to talk about his or her success, Elli would jump in at the first opportunity or even interrupt the speaker to begin her own monologue on a similar success she had. If you were to ask Elli if she considered herself self-centered, she would probably deny it vehemently.

Although Elli may be unaware of the distaste she generates

among her acquaintances, many do recognize how socially unwelcome self-centeredness is and consequently rank it their first and foremost fear.

2. Phony

For men in general, "phony" was the most unwelcome label in this group, ranking first in all men's samples from college onward.

For both men and women, the label "phony" continued to grow in importance, leaping to its peak among women over forty. Two out of every three women over forty marked phony as ranking in concern for them.

Figure 22
COMPARISON OF RESPONSES TO "PHONY" LABEL BETWEEN FEMALES AND MALES
(weighted scores given)

Category	High School	College Age	Young Adults	Over Forty	Total
Females	15	22	21	30	88
Males	17	21	22	23	83

To be phony covers a broad range of meanings. When we asked people what phony means to them, here are some of the replies we received: false, fake, pretense, not genuine, empty, unreal, untrue, fraud, pretender, bogus, artificial, imitation, counterfeit, sham, charlatan, imposter, liar, cheat, misrepresenter, fraudulent, reproduction, a copycat.

Men are expected to compete and achieve in business, in sports, in relationships. How often does the businessman have to "fake it"? Making a presentation before the board, he has to appear calm and collected, when inside he feels like a frightened child. He hasn't really studied and digested the report, yet he's expected to sell the ideas it contains to the new clients. Is life in the business world like a poker game in which bluffing goes on constantly? Whose bluff will be called? Who will get away with it?

One premise commonly held by those who fear they will be seen as phony is that a job well done must take tremendous time and effort. If the job was easy, must they deny that it was well done, important, or authentic?

For example, Jeremy denied he was a good actor because it wasn't difficult for him to act. Because he had a natural flair for acting and did not find it a painful process, he felt he had no right to claim the title "actor." He felt he would be seen as a phony by any real actor because a real actor would have worked a lot harder than he did. "I haven't really earned the right to the name," he explained. "What you actually have in me is a clever phony. My success is a fluke. A real actor eats, sleeps, and lives acting. It is his whole life."

Jeremy is another product of early labeling that has long since become internalized. Again and again, despite his successes, his self-confidence never truly grows, and his label stays internally stuck. Jeremy no longer greatly fears being labeled a phony by others, however, because he has already given himself the label many times.

How do people come to feel they're phony? Again and again, the label "phony" seems to be associated with a loss of self-confidence.

Andrea pursued a master's degree in psychology at an innovative university. Professors encouraged students to write theses that were creative and experiential, rather than traditional academically researched papers. In her own clinical work, Andrea was very innovative, and her professor encouraged her to write about what she was doing in play therapy with educationally handicapped children.

Andrea's husband, Philippe, a traditionalist academic educator, refused to read her master's thesis, saying it wasn't a thesis. "It can't be," he said disdainfully, "because it was not done in the proper way of research papers."

What Andrea heard was her husband calling her a phony. It jarred her self-image. It frightened her to think that other people might react in the same way. It made her feel as though she really didn't deserve her degree. Perhaps she should not show her thesis to anyone else, lest they recognize that she was not truly educated.

After working with a therapist, she began to realize she had been giving away the right to define who she was to her husband, among others.

"I assumed other people had a deeper knowledge than I did," she explained. "I denied my own inner core voice in favor of my husband's judgment and that of others. My inner core voice was affirming what I did as valuable, and I was ready to deny that voice in favor of an outer voice."

3. Cruel

Among men and women "cruel" is the third most heavily weighted variable. This is perhaps one of the most surprising findings in our survey. Though the meaning of the word *cruel* was left vague, it is clear that it engenders significant concern in many people.

According to our sample, almost three out of every five high school girls perceive themselves as cruel, and fear that others will notice their cruelty and speak of it either to their faces or behind their backs.

Figure 23
RANKING OF INNER-QUALITY LABELS FEARED BETWEEN HIGH SCHOOL GIRLS AND BOYS

Rank	High School Girls (N=48)	Weighted Scores	High School Boys (N=46)	Weighted Scores
1	Self-centered	33	Self-centered	26
2	Cruel	23	Cruel	17
3	Phony	15	Phony	17
4	Lazy	7	Stingy	12
5	Superficial	6	Boastful	11
6	Stingy	5	Lazy	9
7	Boastful	5	Superficial	4
8	Immoral	4	Immoral	3

Among the high school boys, the proportion marking "cruel" as a ranked concern was more than two out of every five.

In our college sample, more men than women seem to be concerned about being labeled cruel. For both groups, the concern is quite strong.

As people grow older, at least in our sample, concern about this label seems to lessen somewhat, though it never disappears. (See Table A-5 in the Appendix.)

What does it mean to hear oneself called cruel? Some of our respondents' comments were: vicious, caustic, sarcastic, snide, critical, raw, unfeeling, rough, coarse, fierce, savage, hard-hearted, inhumane, barbarous, without pity, tormenting, vexing, enjoying the pain, suffering, and failure of others, sadistic, without mercy, compassion, or kindness, causing grief and distress.

We suspect that many parents who scold or spank a child in public wonder if the world sees them as cruel and heartless.

Rosalyn's mother was visiting from the Midwest. They were driving along Skyline Drive on a glorious October day ablaze with fall colors. It was a lovely time to be together. Unfortunately, Rosalyn's two daughters, aged three and five, were much more into sibling rivalry than quietly watching pretty leaves. The children continued to fight, cry, tattle on each other, and beg mommy to intercede against the other. This was fairly typical of their attention-seeking behavior, especially when their mother was talking with someone else. And grandmother was no exception.

"I really wanted to stop the car and spank them both," said the young mother, "since all my pleas and gentle reasoning went absolutely unheeded. But I didn't because I didn't want my mother to see me having to discipline my children for fear she would see my act as cruel."

Finally, when it became impossible for Rosalyn to endure the irritating disturbances any longer, she pulled the car off to the side of the road, opened the back door, took out her two fighting daughters, and spanked them both. Then she "laid down the law" and put them back into their seats.

"No matter what my mother thought, I just had to do it," she explained. "After the children were back in the car my mother said to me with a sigh of relief, 'Thank goodness! I thought you were *never* going to get around to doing that.' "

Rosalyn was surprised to hear her mother's response. What Rosalyn thought would appear cruel to her mother, instead seemed very reasonable to her, something in fact she feared her daughter was incapable of doing. Because of what her mother-neighbor might say, Rosalyn had been willing to forego her own right to spend time with her mother without the constant interference of her children.

Cruelty seems to be associated with emotional matters, too. Teasing, tormenting, name-calling, and other emotionally hurtful activities are often associated with cruelty in friendships. Hurting someone's feelings is often seen as being cruel. An inordinate fear of hurting someone's feelings or of being cruel may constrict authenticity, interfere with honesty, integrity, and spontaneity, and distort one's perception of others.

4. Superficial

Though "superficial" ranks fourth in the general lineup, this variable evokes strong concern in women after college, tripling in importance over women's high school levels.

For the men in our sample, the increase in concern for this label grows from a low weighted score of four in high school to a high of eighteen in men over forty. (See Table A-5 in the Appendix.)

Evidently, as men and women grow older they recognize their own lack of human depth and fear that others will notice it, too. Humans are expected to grow wiser as they grow older. Perhaps one consolation is that a part of wisdom means realizing how much we don't know. In any case, being considered deep and profound is very desirable among maturing adults, and the thought that others consider us shallow or superficial is very threatening to many of us.

"When somebody calls me superficial or shallow," said one

woman over forty, "the implications are I don't love very deeply, I don't care very deeply, I don't think very deeply, I don't feel very deeply."

A man who feared being called superficial said that to him the label would mean, "The information I have, the values I proclaim, the things I talk about have little significance. I have a sense that if anyone really probed my knowledge of politics, religion, and world affairs they would discover I have only a thin layer of information. I imagine others are more knowledgeable and deeper than I am."

To others, superficial means "dealing only with the apparent and obvious," "concerned only with externals and outward appearance," "being weak, glossy, slick, and transparent," and "to know a little bit about a lot of things."

Another aspect of the superficial label involves its connection with being uncommitted. Any serious and deep person should be truly committed, goes the logic, so to call someone superficial is to challenge their ability to be responsible and committed. A priest told us his bishop had called him in and asked the priest if he had ever truly committed himself to his priestly work.

"I had been a priest in his diocese for twenty-six years," the priest explained to us, "and I had been very hard working in the ministry, though not in a way my bishop approved of. Even though I felt I had been a committed priest, the strong, accusatory nature of his question led me to wonder if I really knew what true commitment was. It was startling how quickly that man could undermine my own sense of myself."

People sensitive about the "superficial" label often compare themselves to others. Two women friends decided they would like to build a closer relationship with their out-of-town parents. One began phoning her parents every week and writing letters every few days. The other, who got around to writing only once a month, judged herself shallow and uncommitted compared to her friend.

It is natural to be more conscious of one's superficiality as one grows older. Psychologists agree that growth happens in spirals. People never really finish dealing with an issue such as honesty or sincerity or anger or love, but the issue keeps coming back to be faced on ever deeper levels of the growth spiral.

When at age forty or forty-five you look back at your earlier expressions of love and friendship, you realize you do not act today the way you used to. A maturing has happened. Those with children will recognize that care of children used to involve a lot of helping, feeding, dealing with illness, chauffeuring—things that didn't require any significant depth in communication. When the children no longer need your constant care as much, parental roles can feel very superficial. However, if you look closely at this situation, the challenge is to relate to children on a new, even deeper level.

After forty, people begin to go psychologically inward. There is a move toward introspection. For many, it is one of the first times of awareness of how little they have looked at their feelings, their motivation, values, meaning, and goals—how much of what they did in life was done out of expectation; how much involved simply filling a role and doing what everyone else was doing.

After forty, too, comes the awareness that I am finite, that I can't know about everything in depth. I realize there are only a few areas of life that truly interest me, and that is where I want to put my energies. So I must make choices about where I am to seek depth. Rather than say I have been superficial, I can say that I am moving into greater depth in certain areas.

Just as concern for depth increases with age, so concern about physical attractiveness decreases with age. "Beauty is only skin deep" is a saying people support more strongly as they grow older. While this saying is often used to comfort those who don't appear physically beautiful, it also indicates that people as they grow older are generally more interested in competence and experience than in superficial beauty. Also, for older people, the meaning of "beauty" has probably changed, deepened and expanded, and so has the experience of appreciation.

5. Lazy

For both men and women, this unwelcome label evoked most concern among our college-student sample.

Across all age groups, "lazy" is a label found more undesirable by men than by women. Almost one out of every two college men in our survey feared this label enough to rank it in the questionnaire. And men over forty seemed three times more concerned about being called lazy than women over forty, almost none of whom feared this label.

Everyone we talked to had a very strong sense of what it meant to be called lazy. Some emphasized the lack of industriousness with expressions like unproductive, averse to work, unwilling to work, won't do his fair share of work, and sitting around doing nothing. Others emphasized the lack of energy involved in laziness with expressions like slow, sluggish, slothful, indolent, and inactive. Still others associated lazy with being late, tardy, slow to begin.

One mother pointed out a subtle aspect of the way we use the label "lazy." "I think we often call people lazy when they're not doing what we'd like them to be doing at this time. For example, when I feel my daughter should be doing homework and she's not, I tend to call her lazy."

Also, it is wise to remember that hard work and busyness is a hallmark of our culture. As a result, since almost every one of us has been labeled lazy at times, the power of the label may have lost much of its force—except, of course, in the work world, where competition is still a significant factor.

One woman explained how her neighbors controlled each other by using the lazy label.

> When I first moved to Lynnbrook Lane, my next-door neighbor came over to say hello and to tell me what a lazy neighbor had lived here before me. She didn't keep her yard up, I was told, she didn't keep the ivy out of her trees, she didn't keep the honeysuckle back, and she really didn't spend time talking with her neighbors either. She assured me that the neighbors had all noticed these matters. Now I'm afraid I'll be seen as lazy if I don't keep my yard clean,

> car clean, house clean, children clean; if I don't prune my roses, plant my flower beds, or wash my windows. Today my leaf-covered lawn is trumpeting my laziness to all who pass by.

The implication here is I assume neighbors know how I should be using my time better than I do.

6. Immoral

Although the label "immoral" had low concern in our general sample, the statistics showed some interesting dynamics.

Among the high school group it ranked of lowest concern for both boys and girls. Only about one youngster in seven even bothered to mark this label for any rank. Not a single high school boy marked "immoral" of first concern, and only one high school girl marked it of first concern.

Figure 24
COMPARISON OF "IMMORAL" LABEL FEARS
BETWEEN FEMALES AND MALES
(weighted scores given)

Category	High School	College Age	Young Adults	Over Forty	Total
Females	4	10	8	6	28
Males	3	10	4	18	35

Among women, concern for being labeled immoral reached its peak during college years; almost one college female out of three marked it of ranked concern.

Among men, concern over being labeled immoral is just as high as females during college years. But, interestingly, among the men over forty in our sample, fear of being called immoral almost doubles. In the final tally, "immoral" ranked second only to the label "phony" in importance for these men. We are not sure what this particular group understood by the word *immoral*. For example, although certainly many associate immoral with sexual issues, many also associate immoral with unjust business practices, cheating, unethical dealings, kickbacks, lying, and other forms of dishonesty.

When we asked respondents to offer other expressions for immoral, most suggested words with sexual connotations: lewd, obscene, licentious, depraved, dissolute, profligate, unchaste, shameless, dirty, filthy, scandalous, vulgar, crass, immodest in dress and behavior, enjoying pornography, living in sin, seamy, seductive, suggestive, and cheap. However, there were some who suggested expressions not necessarily sexually oriented, such as unjust, crooked, corrupt, a cheat, unethical, a crook.

A young woman, married but separated from her husband, had been living in an apartment complex of all married couples. They presumed she was married, though they had never seen her husband. When people asked her about her marital status, she told them she was married but her husband was away. She admitted to us she felt rejected by her husband and was too embarrassed to say she was separated.

One of the young men from the office where she worked used to drop her off at her apartment on his way home. She usually invited him in for a Coke or a beer before he went on to his own home. He was a single man who lived with his parents.

One of her neighbors put an anonymous note in her mailbox quoting the Bible and accusing her of adultery.

"I had no way to defend myself, no way to explain, and no specific person to explain things to," she said. "I was mortified, embarrassed, frightened. I could imagine every neighbor's eyes on me and thinking adultery. I wouldn't let my co-worker bring me home anymore and took the bus instead. But I still didn't know how to clear my name. The neighborhood that had felt friendly for the lonely and abandoned young woman I was no longer felt friendly. I felt utterly rejected."

Sex, Shame, and the Neighbors

We asked for reactions to our "Neighbors Questionnaire" from a married woman who was involved in behavioral research, and who was also at the time having a clandestine sexual affair with a professor at the university. She found the questionnaire very interesting but said she wished it had contained the category "immoral." (Ironically, the category "immoral" was very clearly present in the questionnaire, *but she hadn't noticed it.*) "People really fear being labeled sexually immoral," she insisted.

If she felt strongly that people would fear being called immoral, our respondents didn't support her. Only the men-over-forty group seemed to express any noticeable concern over the label, and we couldn't be sure whether their concern was about being seen as cheating their corporations, cheating the IRS, or cheating on their wives.

Trying to explain this lack of response to the "immoral" category has been a puzzling challenge. We found a number of elements to consider.

First, it is clear that *many people are concerned about keeping neighbors from knowing their sexual activities, immoral or not.* For example, in therapeutic sessions one hears comments like the following: "What if people find out that I'm gay?" "I don't dare let my parents catch me looking at sexy magazines." "What if the other women in the office knew my husband left me and was seeing another woman?" "I wonder if my partner can tell that I feel sexually awkward." "What if he told friends that I was frigid?" "What would my family say if they knew that I had an abortion?" "I don't want my father to know that I'm sexually active." And so on. It is possible that those in a position of being labeled sexually immoral, such as the young behavioral researcher having an extramarital affair, are very conscious of the label, whereas those who are not in this position remain unconcerned.

Second, it is clear that today *many people simply do not associate the terms* moral *or* immoral *with their sexual activity.* For many contemporary people, sex, other than that which is exploitative, is viewed as a pleasurable experience involving genital arousal enjoyed by one, two, or more consenting persons. In contrast, a woman over fifty years old recited a list of ten "don'ts" that defined "good girls" in the 1950s when she was in college: "Good girls don't smoke, don't drink, don't talk or laugh too loudly, don't use vulgar language, don't flirt (at least not noticeably), don't dress provocatively, don't dance too closely, don't let boys go 'too far,' don't go out with divorced men (let alone married men), and don't have sex outside of marriage." How strange such admonitions sound to young, contemporary ears.

Third, another factor that seems to influence questionnaire response is the *wide range of almost contradictory attitudes found in ordinary homes toward sexually related matters.* In some homes, for example, talk of sex is acceptable; in others it is taboo. Although in certain contexts virginity among unmarried children is honored, in others it is put down and even ridiculed. In some homes, magazines such as *Playboy* or *Penthouse* may be found along with other contemporary magazines; in other homes, such magazines would be forbidden or kept hidden. With such diversity, who can define sexual impropriety?

Fourth, in conversations with people who talked about their neighbor fears concerning sexuality, words like *shame* and *embarrassment* kept cropping up again and again. What we suspect is at work here is not only a fear of being labeled sexual or immoral by neighbors, but two other underlying fears: fear of shame and fear of exposure. For many, the *fear of shame* predominates in sexual situations. Shame involves intense discomfort, and people who know the feeling want to avoid it. According to Washington, D.C., psychiatrist Henry P. Ward, *shame, a very unpleasant emotional state, is experienced whenever a shortcoming of mine is revealed to me or to another.* A shortcoming happens when I fail to live up to the goals and ideals I have currently set for myself. In my current ideal self, there may be many ideals associated with sex, for example, "I am not a sexually promiscuous person." "I am not sexually attracted to members of my own sex." "My children are protected from knowing the times when I am sexually active with my spouse." "Mature adults (like me) do not masturbate." "I do not do things (sexually) that would be disapproved of by my family, my friends, my neighbors, or my church." "I am not a person given to pleasure." I am a person who never loses (sexual) control and who never abandons my reason." Whenever I experience a failure in living up to any of these personal ideals, I am likely to experience shame.

Fifth, *fear of exposure* is also involved in sexual activity. In our culture, sex is a secret, personal, and private matter. Except for the small percentage of public exhibitionists, people find that to be exposed in any way generates uncomfortable feelings. "I would feel embarrassed if someone saw my husband put his hand on my breast," said a woman. "If we were alone and he did it, I would delight in it," she explained. "However, if he did the same thing while anybody else was present in the room, I'd be very embarrassed." To take another example, in a group of women discussing sexual dos and don'ts, seven out of ten had the experience of "hearing our mothers say 'stop that' to our fathers when our fathers wanted to kiss our mothers in front of us." In our culture, *sexuality* and *privacy* are almost synonymous terms. For example, even in *Penthouse*'s "Forum," which publishes letters people write describing their sexual exploits and fantasies in explicitly erotic detail, most of the letter-writers are unwilling to have their stories linked with their names; more often than not a letter ends with the signature "Name withheld by request."

Sixth, when fear of shame and fear of exposure are joined, people tend to defend themselves by *denial*. Actions that produce shame are most often kept secret. We would like to keep our shame from the awareness of others, even from ourselves, if possible. Meredith remembered wishing she could have denied her sexuality when she was sixteen.

> My father made some innuendos about me being very sexy. I was horrified, partially because I knew it was true. In his anger, he said I'd probably be willing to go out with anyone who had a penis. I thought it was horrible and disgusting for my father to say such a thing. My reaction was so strong because as an adolescent I was experiencing strong sexual urges. With that accusation, I felt that I had been "caught" and "seen" by my father for what I was. I was embarrassed beyond belief, and wished I could have denied my sexual feelings.

That someone would discover our shame and make it public is a terrifyingly destructive prospect, and we do everything possible to avoid exposure.

Meredith's story points out the extreme pain experienced by persons when their shame is revealed *involuntarily*. Involuntary exposure means that my shame is no longer concealed and under my control, but is revealed and in the hands of my neighbors. I realize it can be used by them to devalue me and I want to avoid this at all cost. As Henry Ward put it, "The threat of exposure of hidden aspects of the self can marshal enough energy not only to keep things hidden, but also to keep even the question of their revelation from ever being raised. The ego acts as if involuntary exposure is the 'ultimate weapon' [of the neighbors]."

In summary, despite the fact that the behavioral researcher believed "immoral" would be a popular response, it turned out not to be so among our sample. We suggested six factors that might help explain our questionnaire results. Our feeling is that, although a few people might possess enough courage and ego-strength voluntarily to acknowledge their immorality, sexual or otherwise, the rest are either unconcerned, don't view their sexual activity as immoral, prefer to keep their sexuality a private matter, or fear shame and exposure so strongly that they would pay any price, or do almost anything (even denial), to keep the sexual and shameful parts of their lives hidden from view, sometimes even from their own view of themselves.

7. Stingy

Being called stingy seems to be of concern only to young males. High school boys seem most sensitive to this label, and college males next most concerned about it. For all other groups in our sample, this label seems to be of little importance.

What does this label mean to people? Some responses include: unwilling to pay one's fair share, cheap, avoiding spending any money, greedy with money, closefisted, not generous with time or money, a withholding person, ungiving and unsharing, uncharitable, and miserly.

Fear of being called stingy is typical of the psychological dynamics with unwelcome labels in general. People who fear being called stingy often overreact by a determination to be generous, for example, doing more than their share, overtipping, insisting on picking up the entire bill, giving gifts more expensive or more often than necessary.

However, one of two things tend to happen with people determined to be overly generous to prove they are not stingy. Either they back away from their generous promises and never really make the generous gesture; in this case, they may end up convinced that they truly are stingy. Or they carry out the overly generous gesture, and instead of feeling good about themselves, they feel exploited, ripped off, as if the people they feared would label them stingy had really forced them to act in this overly generous way. Along with these angry feelings often comes the fear that deep down they are really ungenerous. In either case, trying to prove the falsity of the unwelcome label only mires them in it much more deeply.

One woman over forty we talked to told a story about being born into a stingy family. Even though the family could have afforded to buy new things for their children, it was more likely the children would get hand-me-downs or damaged articles.

> Everything we got seemed to be secondhand or second-rate, even our Christmas gifts. When I was eleven, I told my parents I wanted only one gift for Christmas, a very special, big, and pretty doll that I could save for my own children. When Christmas came, there was indeed a big doll under the tree for me. The doll had been pretty, but had been damaged, because one side of her face was all cracked and discolored. She was obviously bought at discount because she was damaged, and she was obviously not a doll I would be proud to show to my children. In this gift, my parents hadn't been stingy just toward me, but they were already being stingy toward my children. To my young mind, they were already passing on a tradition of stinginess to their as-yet-unborn grandchildren. Even the symbolic message of their gift saddened me.

In talking further with the woman, we discovered a number of psychological effects of the "stingy" label. First, she never stopped being aware of the stinginess of her parents and never stopped resenting it. Second, it caused her to be stingy with herself. Even after she married a well-to-do man, she carried to extremes her tendency to buy the least expensive things for herself. Third, with regard to buying things for her children and other people she became inconsistent. "I would be drawn to buy a bargain," she explained, "but then part of me would accuse me of being stingy. Then out of fear of this label I would overreact by buying more than was needed or better than was needed."

Usually she overindulged her own children. And once when trying to decide on a gift to send her mother she couldn't stop at buying a quality coat for her, but felt obliged to buy her also a hat, gloves, purse, and scarf to match. "It felt like if I neglected to get her any one of these accessories, I would be stingy."

8. Boastful

Among the inner-quality labels, "boastful" evoked the least concern from our sample respondents in general. There were two observations, however.

The first is that high school boys seemed most sensitive to this label. One out of every three of our sample of males in high school marked "boastful" a name they worry about being called by others.

The second is that in the over-forty age group, the women in our sample have almost five times more sensitivity to being labeled "boastful" than men.

Many of the synonyms for boastful given by our respondents were reminiscent of adolescent language, for example, stuck up, tooting your own horn, big-headed, thinks he's hot stuff, big-mouthed, braggart, show-off, conceited, and puffed up.

Jeff is an adolescent with a bountiful head of hair. He does spend a lot of time caring for it and does take pride in the fact that he has nice hair. He's also afraid his sisters and classmates might accuse him of being proud and boastful of his hair, so he is very conscious never to mention his hair and is uncomfortable when anyone else does.

So strong is the fear of being labeled boastful that lots of people, like Jeff, depreciate what they are proud of, especially when they are confronted by someone's compliment of them.

Some people even feel boasting causes bad luck, and that they risk losing what they brag about.

What are the things people boast about? Their intelligence, talents, accomplishments, good looks, family, home, car, clothing, friends, connections, jobs, possessions, collectibles, and opportunities. People tend to brag about things that others couldn't easily obtain or match.

People have a secret fear of being different from everyone else when this difference might exclude them in some way from belonging to the group. Boasting is a way of people presenting themselves as different and therefore putting themselves outside the group. People bothered by a fear of being called boastful find it difficult to recognize their uniqueness as the gift it truly is and to take ownership of it. The presumption is that if the neighbors saw me own all these goods, qualities, or accomplishments they would resent me, see me as different from them, and perceive me as stepping outside the group norm. In short, the fear is I either don't fit in or won't be allowed in.

Psychologically, it is necessary to own your potentials. It is important to allow yourself the fullness of your accomplishments and life. People unable to own either their positive or negative qualities, their creativity and accomplishments, or their potential for destructiveness, really limit their access to growth and development. It seems, if they can't affirm the totality of their potential, they are obliged to diminish themselves.

PART THREE

How to Deal with the Fear

CHAPTER 10

Working Through the Fear with a Therapist: The Story of Catherine

Psychologically, most people are only moderately affected by fear of what neighbors might say about them. However, there are some who are so crippled by and trapped in neighbor fear that they need professional help to work through it. Although most people should be able to discard much of their unnecessary fear of what the neighbors might say by utilizing the suggestions presented in Part Three of this book, the woman whose story we present here needed therapeutic help.

A Missing Identity

At forty-two, Catherine was still slim and attractive. Her light brown hair, parted on the side, fell to her shoulders in a soft wave. With a heart-shaped face, blue eyes, and a clear complexion, she appeared a decade younger than she was. She seemed very quiet and at peace in her body, and a natural grace belied the self-consciousness that plagued her life. When she talked, she used her hands.

She was putting her signature at the bottom of a note when she first came for counseling, and she hesitated as she wrote her name.

"After all these years, my hand does not know how to write my own name," she said. "I have to spell Catherine consciously in my mind, letter by letter, as I write it. It's as if it isn't even my own name, though I've been writing it for nearly forty years."

She hadn't taken charge of her own internal identity. She had no consistent, realistic image of herself. It seemed the outer world had simply put an identity on her.

"My name was given to me," she went on, "and I guess I just put it on over whoever I was underneath. Like when I was a child at Halloween and I decided to go as a gypsy. When I knocked at somebody's door, they didn't say 'Hello, Catherine,' they said, 'Hello, gypsy.' They didn't know who was under the mask till I told them. And even if they knew, they went along with the game and called me by the mask I wore. It feels like I've been wearing a Catherine mask for years. What's even worse is that when people say things about me—that I'm a good mother or a bad mother, a good friend or a bad friend—I don't know if it is the *real me* they're talking about. I'm confused about who I am. Even if what people say about me feels wrong and hurts me, I don't know how to say it's *not really me* they're talking about."

Catherine realized that a lot of her life was made up of masks and costumes, what psychiatrist Carl Jung called the persona. On the one hand, it was a big step for Catherine just to realize how pervasive her persona mask was. On the other hand, she found it somewhat frightening not to be in touch consciously with her real personal qualities. At times, she could not seem to affirm or deny the image of herself that the people in her life reflected back to her.

"Sometimes people tell me I'm a good mother or a good friend, but I don't know if those compliments really belong to me. What's scariest is when someone like one of my children calls me a bad mother; then acts as if I were really bad."

When asked how someone might do that, she answered, "By avoiding me, by not spending time with me, by talking negatively about me to friends, by forgetting my birthday and Mother's Day, by not saying 'I love you' to me. But the scary part is that *I don't know that I'm not what the person calls me,* particularly if that person treats me as if the negative things he or she says about me are true. I easily lose touch with the reality of who I am."

Catherine didn't seem to know who she was deep down, and since she couldn't hear the voice inside her, who would know who she truly was, she was unable to stay in touch with her own reality. For example, she was apt to think of herself as talking too much, sounding stupid, uninformed, or boring.

Without an Inner Perspective

She recalled a fantasy she had about herself:

> It's like whoever shines a spotlight on me and says, "I see you," defines how I see myself. I see myself from their perspective because I don't have my own inner perspective. Imagine a darkened stage, and on this stage there's a person who doesn't know where to stand or what part to play. That's me. Then a spotlight suddenly appears on me and a voice says, "I see you, and you're not a very kind person." I get frightened and I want to get out of that glaring light, rather than stand there and say, "You're wrong. I am a kind person, at least most of the time." But I don't stay and confront the voice. Instead, I scurry away. And then another spotlight finds me. The person focusing this spotlight might say, "You're stingy." I run away again, and again another spotlight finds me. I keep running from one light to another. I don't stand there secure in my own reality and say who I am.
>
> Not all the things people say about me are bad either. Some say nice things. But when someone turns their spotlight on me and says, "You're very thoughtful and patient," I still don't know how to stand there and say, "That's me." Instead, I run from that spotlight too, because I don't know if that's me either. I'm just as afraid and untrusting of the good names as I am of the unwelcome ones.

Catherine didn't know how to deal with the outer voices, or how to balance what she heard in the outer world with what she heard in the inner world because she could not keep in touch with her inner world enough to check out its congruency with outer reality. Once she could learn to evaluate people's comments from within, the people with the spotlights could be helpful to her. At present, she couldn't use their information helpfully. She was still too unsure of herself to be able to make use of what she heard from the outside world in ways that would be productive for her own growth. It would be ideal for her to be able to confront the voices of others—her children, for example, who had called her stingy. It would be a great stride in growth if she could say, "I'm not really stingy. Maybe at times I seem too careful how I spend money, but most times I'm very generous. I'd like you to remember some of the generous things I've done, too. Right now I'm not able to be generous in the way you'd like me to be. But maybe I can find a way to be generous now, too. It's helpful to know that you experience me as being stingy right now." But Catherine's self-confidence and self-image were still far from that place of confrontation. Catherine wished she would not be confused or misled by the outer voices, the voices she called her neighbors.

"Some of them are the people who live in my neighborhood, but most of them are the people at home and work, including my children, my husband, my parents, my brothers and sisters, my in-laws."

Childhood in a Critical Family

There was also a whole generation of people associated with Catherine's parents whose voices at one time or another were important to her and whose opinions she and her parents listened to attentively. "There was a Mrs. Brooks, who lived next door when I was a little girl," she explained. "Many times I would hear my mother say, 'Catherine, you can't go out of the house looking like that! I'd be mortified if the neighbors saw you.' And in my imagination I would picture Mrs. Brooks looking horrified, with raised eyebrows and a hand covering her gasping mouth, as I walked out of the house in a bathing suit, or some outfit my mother thought looked immodest or silly. So, when I go out the door of my home now, I'm still acutely conscious of how I look, imagining the neighbors would be horrified if I weren't careful about my appearance."

When Catherine was asked what she thought this experience meant to her, she replied perceptively, "Of course, it's me who would feel mortified. Or maybe it's still my mother who would feel mortified. As a child, I didn't know someone could be mortified by a neighbor's disapproval, but my mother taught me that she could be. Maybe I'm still trying to protect my mother from being mortified."

Currently, Catherine said she had trouble listening to others when she was anxious and had difficulty remembering names of people to whom she was introduced. When in groups she became so concerned about how she was perceived by others that she lost awareness of them as individuals; their personalities didn't come across to her very clearly. Catherine said that when she was a little girl she was very friendly and, in fact, recalled getting scolded for being overly talkative. She remembered being teased about her chattiness by her older sister, who used to say, "Catherine talks just to hear her head roar." Though Catherine minded the accusation, she didn't think it ever kept her from talking, though it did make her self-conscious.

Catherine came from an ethnic, working-class, Roman Catholic family who lived in a large midwestern city. A product of parochial schools from the first grade on, she did remarkably well in school and won a full scholarship to college. She never went on to college, however, because at high school graduation a job she was offered seemed more attractive to her parents than the scholarship to college. Catherine didn't question the accuracy of her parents' judgments.

"I never felt I belonged in my family," she added. "I learned to fit in anyplace, but I never really belonged anyplace. Because I was able to adapt to any situation, I looked as though I fit in; but down deep it never felt real."

Catherine said there had been much emphasis in her family on what "the relatives" did and thought. They seemed to be the most influential neighbors. She described a very critical family, where parents, siblings, and other relatives got their own sense of being right (righteous) by finding faults and flaws in other people. According to her, her family did a lot of negative labeling.

"In our neighborhood there was a popular young girl named Millie who dated a lot," Catherine explained, "and my father often referred to her as a floozie, and I understood that to be something bad. I found my father's attitude confusing because when my father described my two cousins, who were of the same age as Millie and dated desirable young men just as frequently as she did, he called them 'popular and going to make a good marriage.' I couldn't figure out why Millie was called a floozie, while the cousins were proudly called popular."

Catherine had also been confused about what to do with her own attractiveness, the friendliness and warmth that naturally drew people to her. She tried very hard to get labeled popular and not a floozie by her father and the relatives, but she had no way to measure her success since they gave her no clear feedback. Also, she was confused because she liked the warm and chatty Millie, who took time to laugh and talk with her, a thing her "popular" cousins didn't do, even though they went to the same school.

Catherine was clearly someone upon whom fear of what the neighbors might say had a powerfully destructive effect. When asked if she had a sense of how she came to be so dependent on what her family and the neighbors said, she replied, "My parents were always preoccupied by what the neighbors and relatives might be saying about us. They acted as though the neighbors were watching us all the time. If we were on our porch or in the yard, they presumed the neighbors were looking at us, criticizing what we were wearing, judging what we were doing, evaluating what they could overhear us saying." She gave an example.

> I remember my mother almost having a fit when as a ten-year-old I walked home from a movie holding hands with the little boy who lived down the street. She scolded me as

> if holding hands were something awful and offensive to the people in our neighborhood. For my mother, every display of feelings was shocking and disgraceful in the eyes of the neighbors. That attitude had its effects even inside our home. For instance, during an argument in our family everyone was expected to keep their voices down so that the neighbors wouldn't hear. It was as if the neighbors were constantly tuned in on us, consequently we had to be extremely careful of everything we did or said. The assumption was always that the neighbors would be negative and critical.
>
> I remember being spanked as a child, and having my mother tell me she was holding her hand over my mouth "so the neighbors won't hear you cry." At the time I wondered what that meant. Did it mean my mother didn't want the neighbors to know how bad I must be to deserve a spanking? Or did it mean my mother was embarrassed and fearful that the neighbors would think of her as a cruel mother for spanking me?

Catherine became aware of her own "confusion about having to protect this person I was angry at for spanking me from being seen by the neighbors as having spanked me." It was not surprising that Catherine found her situation confusing and frightening. From childhood on, there was no place in her life where she wasn't feeling watched and judged by someone. The watchers became an all-seeing, critical, amorphous force in her life.

An Angering Revelation

Social scientists recognize that one of society's functions is to keep people living according to social expectations. Maintaining law, order, and custom is the shared task of family, church, school, and other institutions of society. The theory is that when people believe they are always being watched by one neighbor or another they will remain well-behaved members of society. Fear of such neighbors may be observed in the extreme by a family like Catherine's.

"I guess I assumed that everyone lived like us," said Catherine.

It was an angering revelation to her to find that not everyone lived so constricted a life and so terrorized by fear of the neighbor's criticism. She was also angry to discover that fear of the neighbors had been enlarged and perpetuated by her own imagination. She was angry that throughout her life she had viewed almost everyone in her world as dangerous and critical instead of potentially helpful, caring, generous, and friendly. As a child, Catherine's trust in the world had been severely damaged. For her, the neighborhood had become a hostile environment, and she could not trust that the world would be a hospitable place in which to grow up. Catherine learned to view the outside world as though it were her critical parents. She internalized their fears of the neighbors, their critical attitudes, their lack of generosity in evaluating others, *and turned them upon herself.*

Some people refer to their fear of neighbors' comments as "sensitivity to others." Among these there are some extremely sensitive ones, like Catherine, who experience the least criticism as very threatening and demoralizing. Many of these sensitive people are able to rebalance their ego-identity—feeling stung at first by the criticism but able to put it back into its proper place in the larger perspective of their life. Catherine, however, could not seem to do that. Only the present moment seemed to have reality for her.

Intellectually, Catherine knew that she was a good and capable person; but on the gut level, the level she lived out of particularly during times of stress and uncertainty, she didn't have a positive self-image to stand upon. In her, that place of self seemed empty. When someone criticized her, she experienced their judgment as completely true, and it got enlarged in her mind until it became the totality of who she was. For example, if someone accused her of being stingy, she felt guilty and had no defense except to run and hide. But even that wouldn't relieve her from the embarrassment of having been seen as stingy. She didn't seem to have the ability to shift to a broader perspective after her first reaction. Instead, she continued to feel as though she had been stingy "unquestionably, thoroughly, totally, and always." Her entire history of generosity would be wiped out. As a result, she would become enormously demoralized and hate herself.

The Work of Therapy

At one level, the therapeutic work with Catherine focused on *building a more affirmative view of her reality.* Capitalizing on the affirmative experiences that came her way enabled her to feel them and begin to internalize them. First, she began to experience success among a group of adults returning to college, and she was able to let herself feel a part of the group instead of separate from them and judged by them. She reported feeling "a lot like the others, and even connected to some of them." Second, Catherine found writing a job resumé another freeing experience. When she read the finished resumé she said to herself, "I'd really like to know that person; she sounds very interesting."

She had a third moment of self-recognition and self-affirmation when, as part of her college program, she was asked to write an essay about herself in terms of the past (where she had come from), the present (as she saw herself now), and the future (what she wanted to do with her life in light of her goals and values). Again, Catherine's ability to see herself described in the written word proved helpful to her, for she was able to read her story as though she were reading someone else's life and vision. Again, she liked the person she read about. In her own words, "I liked that person, then realized it was me. How I wished I could have held onto the good feeling of knowing that likable person was me!"

Moreover, as far as she was concerned, the world of people outside her wasn't consistent in its acceptance and liking of her. She couldn't believe that the person who yesterday said, "I like you," still liked her today. Affirmations didn't seem to get internalized, but criticism did. Her negative self-image remained unshaken even when critical neighbors had a change of heart.

Building Consistency

At a second level in therapy, the task was to reverse her self-critical attitude and help her *begin consistently to think of herself as being liked in contrast to being disliked.* At the beginning of therapy, she mostly thought of herself as simply not being seen at all. "That's the safest feeling," she said. Given her wish, she preferred to hide in the darkness of nonbeing.

Another hallmark of Catherine's personality was that she had no real belief in herself. When she enjoyed successes, she had no way of believing they would continue, no way of believing she could do again what she did yesterday. Each new moment in her life seemed without a history. When she wasn't fearing what the neighbors might say, she felt empty, nonexistent, indifferent. Catherine lacked the experience of making impact. For her, only the neighbors had an impact.

In Catherine, we're talking about someone who is deeply vulnerable because of early ego damage. Her family experience did severe damage to her budding ego through constant criticism and failure to acknowledge her identity in positive ways. Because she received from her family little or no positive feedback, but only negative feedback or an absence of feedback, there was no positive sense of self to mold. From them she knew only the experience of rejection of her self.

Conscious Affirmations from Within

A third task in therapy was to get Catherine *consciously building affirmations of identity from within.* When asked if there was something positive about herself that she could acknowledge, she replied after a few moments of thought, "I think I'm a kind person most of the time, but I don't think anyone notices." The following week she returned and said that she had been thinking more about the question. "I think I'm also a thoughtful person." In therapy, she was given much reinforcement for owning herself as a kind person and again for affirming herself as a thoughtful person. She was asked to think of some other qualities to add to these.

When she arrived the following week, almost before sitting down, she said she had been thinking about herself as kind and thoughful, and how it was true. She began giving examples of kind and thoughtful things she had been doing for people over many years. Most of the session was spent talking about example after example in her life where she had been kind and thoughtful, and where her kindness had been acknowledged by other people as well. In the middle of the therapy session, she added that she thought she was a good listener. There was much laughter during the session, and before she left she announced she thought she had a good sense of humor. For many weeks it was her task consciously to focus on the positive elements of her identity. Bits and pieces of history that confirmed the positive qualities on her list got talked about and thought about.

At times during the therapeutic process, she brought poetry she had written and was able to affirm the creative side of herself. Sometimes she brought books that she liked and she talked about why she liked them. In therapy, she was reflected as an intelligent person whose opinions, ideas, and values were respected, and she learned little by little to respect and enjoy them in herself.

As therapy progressed, Catherine learned to be at home with internal self-affirmation. She learned to hear her own self-valuing above the voices of her critical inner and outer neighbors. Because of severe childhood ego damage, Catherine's inner self-affirmation process would probably involve a lifetime struggle, but at least she was getting to the place where she was not being emotionally devastated and having her equilibrium destroyed by a single negative comment.

Testing Reality

A fourth level of her therapy program included *discrimination and reality-testing.* One question she learned to ask over and over was: How much of my energy and concern does this issue really deserve? Instead of treating every person's possible comments about her as huge and threatening, she learned to decide where to put her energy and time. With practice, she learned to recognize how much power over her she had been giving to even the most insignificant persons in her life. Reality-testing reminded her that perhaps in some relationships, where intimacy was not called for, she would decide it would be wise for her to keep distance and not reveal her deeper feelings.

Finally, she learned about her need to discriminate and reflect on her own motives and the motives of others. She discovered she sometimes acted in ways that were harmful to relationships. For example, she found that her general lack of trust in others blocked her capacity for close friendships. On the other hand, there were places where not trusting might make good sense and caution would be wise.

Catherine's therapy seemed to be successful inasmuch as she had begun developing a mature and discriminating sense of what was appropriate in relationships and in her own behavior. This sense included an enjoyment of her capacities and an acceptance of her limitations. For example, she grew more comfortable accepting her own dependency needs and in doing so actually became less dependent. She realized how much she had relied on the outside world for feedback and in making decisions about her life.

Getting in Touch with Her Self

At a fifth level of therapy, Catherine was encouraged to be more *nurturing of her own intuitions, ideas, choices, and values*. As she realized she had values, wants, goals, and a vision for herself, she found it easier to make choices for herself because she could see how they emerged out of her own sense of self. One of her tasks during therapy had been to get in touch with her values, wants, and goals; to know, explore, and name them over and over.

In the future, Catherine will probably always carry the tendency to be supersensitive to what other people say, want, or expect of her; and she will probably continue to have the tendency to want to make choices to please other people. That is part of her personality. She's a person who likes to make other people happy, and she likes that part of her. Her ongoing task will be to remain conscious of her strong desire to please other people, and to manage that tendency. For example, when she finds herself being asked to do something, she will need to stop a moment before agreeing to do it and ask herself, "Do I choose to do this? Is this something I really want to do?" One of the things Catherine agreed to do was to ask for "time to think" when a request was made of her. "Let me think about that, and I'll get back to you" was an expression she felt comfortable using. It may be that over a period of time she will learn automatically to take time to think before she responds, but for a while she will have to train herself consciously to do it. Often during her period of therapy she would forget to stop and think and would slip back into her old pattern. But instead of putting herself down for forgetting, she began to learn to spend her energy reminding herself that she has been changing and will try to remember next time.

During therapy, Catherine began the slow process of revealing her self to herself. She began accepting the wholeness of who she was, integrating the not-so-good and the not-so-bad parts of her. She began to realize that her few moments of selfishness and stinginess were not important in the larger picture. As she said, "Though I don't like the stingy part of myself and don't like anyone to notice it, it's not such a big deal."

It was very freeing for her when she finally realized most people weren't paying close attention to what she did or said. "If they had listened closely," she commented, "they probably still would have thought what I said was okay; but the truth of the matter was they probably weren't listening that closely or critically at all."

So Catherine began to find herself simply among the human race, realizing she couldn't control what the neighbors said about her, realizing also that most neighbors didn't pay much attention to her anyway, and finally, realizing that even if they did it was her right to respond in ways that were true to her nature and in ways that nurtured her self-confidence and self-image.

CHAPTER 11

How to Take Back the Power Over Yourself You May Have Given to the Neighbors

Has fear of what the neighbors might say about you been robbing you of the ability to enjoy what you have, and to be who you are? Do you find fear of your family's and neighbors' opinions weakens your ability to discern your own truth and act on your own values, wants, and rights? Have you been inviting inner neighbors to speak on your behalf and make important decisions for you?

Do you have a hard time listening to the voice of your true self and following your own inner wisdom? Do you find it easier to hang onto your fears than to nourish your hopes; easier to ferret out the negative comments of others and focus on them than to listen for the positive and work at self-development; easier to harbor insults than to live up to a real compliment or the naming of a true gift?

Are you willing to give up power over your life to the neighbors in the hope of being seen as a good guy or a nice woman? Do you find it easier to stay dependent than to assume responsibility for your life? Do you find it easier to preserve the status quo than to accept the possibility that you are called to be something more?

In the following pages, we will suggest five levels of approach for dealing with fear of neighbors' comments, following the five levels of therapeutic work used with Catherine. Though Catherine often needed the therapist's support and guidance in doing the necessary work, most people who are sufficiently motivated to deal with their fear of neighbors' comments can benefit from the activities and themes for reflection we offer here. These suggestions are designed to develop and nurture a change in attitude toward yourself. They may also prove helpful in reconnecting you to your healthy and assertive attitudes whenever you might begin to slip back into old negative and fearful ones.

In beginning a program of self-change, some people tend to take such an all-or-nothing attitude that they fall into the trap of seeing a single slip as a total failure. Researchers Alan Marlatt and Susan Goldstein at the University of Washington discovered two psychological effects that tend naturally to follow any lapse in resolution. They suggest that, after I make a slip, (1) I will tend to feel badly about myself for the slip, and (2) I am likely to begin playing down the importance of my decision or resolution to change. To explain these effects, they suggest that people whose resolves are too demanding may view a violation as undermining their self-image, and rather than lose any more of their self-esteem they prefer to withdraw from their resolution to change.

It is unrealistic to demand of yourself total success as the only measure of success. "It's not all or nothing," Goldstein asserts. "What you're trying to control is an overlearned, almost reflex, habit. You're not a failure if you slip now and then. You're trying to make a difficult change." Because you're trying to make a difficult change, do it step by step, little by little. Enjoy your successes, and forgive yourself when you slip.

Level One: Building a More Balanced View of How You Really Appear to Others

A first step in dealing with fear of neighbors' comments is to strengthen your own self-image by *collecting the affirma-*

tive experiences you have had and are having. Your collection might include the good words you hear from your friends, the compliments you get from your boss, the positive reports and reactions you receive, the successes you have, and any events or encounters that make you feel good about yourself. The stronger your positive self-image grows, the better prepared you will be to face your deeper fears successfully. Avoid having your first confrontation with your most frightening fear.

To begin, try writing, as Catherine did, a strongly positive *resumé of your accomplishments and qualifications,* as if you were applying for a job you really desired. Catherine found this activity very helpful, as she did the following.

Write an affirmative *story about your life,* including (1) where you've come from, (2) where you are now, and (3) where you hope to be—your past, present, and future in the light of your life values and goals. Allow yourself to enjoy the process as you do it, and reflect on ways it can help build your self-image and self-esteem.

With paper and pen, draw up *a list of affirmations others have made about you.* As you write each affirmation, recall a time when it was given to you, and in your imagination relive the experience in depth and detail.

In a similar way, *collect a list of your positive qualities.* As you write each quality, think of a time when that quality was used by you, and in your imagination relive the experience. Any quality you exhibit more than 50 percent of the time deserves to be on your list. A woman whose husband one evening labeled her impatient replied that she was patient at least 80 percent of the time, and for that reason claimed she did not deserve to be called an impatient person. After all, even players with the highest batting averages in major-league baseball get hits only about 40 percent of the time.

To help you get in touch with how you are viewed by others, make two lists. Let the first list contain the names of all the people you can think of who apparently like you, including even those who seem to like you only a little bit. Second, list the people who have clearly and directly acted in ways that indicate they don't like you. After each name on this second list, note the action or words that might prove their personal dislike of you. After completing both lists, share them with a close friend or two whom you trust. Ask for their comments, and compare your perceptions with theirs. Be open to changing your self-perception, and be willing to add other names to your list of people who apparently like you.

Level Two: Building Consistency in Thinking Positively

If you wish to reach the goal of being free of fear of the neighbors, it is important to *develop a strong, positive self-image and maintain it.* Consistency requires discipline and practice. Since you are trying to control and replace unwanted old habits, responses need constant practice if they are going to become habitual. Unless the messages you hear spoken in your deepest self are repeated and strengthened consistently, the old critical inner parent and neighbor messages will reassert their power over you.

It is important to remember that we have a right to find and use healthy ways to nurture our self-confidence and self-image. Although we can't really control what the neighbors say about us, it is consoling to know that most neighbors don't pay much attention to us anyway. Even if they do, we have a right to respond to situations in ways that are true to ourselves. For example, it is important that the neighbors, internal or external, neither coerce you into making decisions against your best interests nor assume the responsibility of making your decisions for you.

To practice building consistency in your self-image, you might begin by explaining to a close friend or two that you want to develop a strong, positive self-image. *Ask your friends to name your positive qualities.* Ask them, too, to tell you instances in which these qualities were apparent to them. As you listen, let your imagination help you relive these experiences and affirm you in those positive qualities. Acknowledging your positive qualities (often difficult for someone with low self-esteem) is easier when you can point to specific moments where you exercised patience, generosity, good judgment, and so on. Collect all your positive qualities, including those from activities in Level One, and *read them aloud to yourself two or more times each day* for at least a week, allowing consciousness of them to sink deeply into your awareness.

Whenever you slip back into fear of how neighbors might respond and feel pressured into saying something you really don't believe, *take the time in private to reaffirm your true belief.* The value of such reaffirmation has been shown by the research of social psychologist Solomon Asch. He recognized that, as a rule, individuals have two important desires: *the wish to be correct* and *the wish to stay in the good graces of other people,* usually by living up to their expectations. In most cases, both these desires may be satisfied by a single action. However, when these two desires are placed in conflict, for example, when everyone but me has a different notion of what is correct, it is likely I will conform *publicly* to the judgments of others, that is, I will verbally agree with everyone else. However, Asch found, such social pressure has little if any effect on the *private* judgments of individuals in conflicts like these. So, even if you outwardly succumb to fear of the neighbors' disapproval, it does not mean your inner values have changed. You may reaffirm them to yourself.

What if, after all your firm resolutions not to be controlled by fear of what neighbors might say, you slip up? For example, you say something you really don't believe or do something you didn't choose to do. Instead of giving up, Daniel Goleman, a senior editor of *Psychology Today,* encourages us to take advantage of our lapses. "A slip is not a disaster," he asserts, "but a clue to the right strategies to apply in the future." *Use a slip as a way to learn to be more effective.* For example, your lapse may give you an insight into what situations are high risk for you, or who among your neighbors seems to have the most power to influence you. You can try to avoid such situations or people in the future. The idea is not to cover up slips or lapses, but to use them as a helpful measure of success.

It is difficult to evaluate success in carrying out overly generalized resolutions such as "I'm not going to let people's comments bother me anymore." More effective programs of change involve resolutions that are *measurable, specific, and realistic,* such as "At the party tonight, if someone makes a comment about me that I think is critical, I will interiorly reaffirm myself as a likable person. If I remember to do this at least 50 percent of the time, I will consider it a success." One value of having *measurable and specific resolutions* is that successes as well as lapses are clearly evident, and thus enable resolvers to measure their improvement. The value of *realistic resolutions* is that they offer strong likelihood of success. Since success breeds success, amassing a series of specific and realistic successes will tend to build self-confidence and a strong, positive self-image.

Level Three: Building Conscious Affirmations of Self-Image from Within

The major thrust of Level Three is *conscious, internal self-affirmation.* While Level One focused on collecting examples of *external affirmation,* and Level Two focused on *building consistency,* the emphasis at this stage involves understanding the ways you react to fear-arousing situations and learning how to use these dynamics to best advantage in shaping a healthy self-image.

There is no doubt that at times the comments neighbors make about us are fear-arousing communications. Howard Leventhal proposed that such messages produce two parallel and independent reactions: one is *to control the inner fears* aroused by the threat, the other is *to cope with the external dangers.* For example, if I hear that some of my fellow professors have been spreading false rumors to the department chairman about my being sexually involved with certain students, I will have two reactions: an inner emotional one, fear at what might happen to my reputation and my job; and an external coping one, which might include facing and acknowledging the danger, adopting adequate means of squelching the rumor, and obtaining additional information from others about how to cope with it. In general, then, in dealing with neighbor fears, I will need to (1) learn to control the inner fears aroused by the threat of negative labeling, and (2) learn to cope with the effects the labeling has on my self-image, and my acceptance and esteem in the community.

How do fears work on us? Leventhal's experimental data suggest that, all other things being equal, the more frightened we are by what we hear or fear hearing, the more likely we are to take positive action to prevent or control the problem. On the other hand, everybody knows that in certain cases a great deal of fear leads to inaction. Why this difference? It seems that in situations of high fear arousal people with high self-esteem are the ones most likely to be moved to action, while low self-esteemers often become paralyzed; but if they are given sufficient time they will eventually initiate coping action. In *The Social Animal,* Elliot Aranson, professor of psychology at the University of California, Santa Cruz, reaffirms this description of low self-esteemers:

> A high-fear communication overwhelms them and makes them feel like crawling into bed and pulling the covers up over their heads. Low or moderate fear is something that they can more easily deal with at the moment they experience it. But, if given time—that is, if it's not essential that they act immediately—they will be more likely to act if the message truly scared the hell out of them.

Practice in self-affirmatively confronting fears plays an important role in changing self-image and building healthy self-esteem. To be able to do inner affirmation successfully requires a knowledge of how your inner parents, inner neighbors, and inner self (or conscience) can work for you.

One activity you might enjoy doing is called a "this-is-your-life fantasy." At a time when you are relaxed and free from immediate pressures, imagine yourself walking down a receiving line of the people whose comments you most fear. But instead of criticizing you, each one speaks to you about the *positive ways in which they have viewed you.* Acknowledge each of their affirmations as you look them in the eye and shake their hand. You may want to play some enjoyable music as background to your fantasy. This activity is a way of meeting some of your inner neighbors in a new light.

It may be helpful to review some of your strongest inner-parent and neighbor messages, to see them also in a new light. Begin by making a list of all the old messages you remember from childhood, messages spoken by parents, relatives, teachers, clergy, and so on. No matter how obviously true or false they now seem, write them down, especially if they evoked anxiety, concern, or fear in you, for example, "I was told I was fat," "I was told I talked too much," "I was told I was selfish." After your list has been compiled, reread those old messages from the following four perspectives. First, make note of those messages that may have been appropriate during childhood but are no longer so; these are the messages that *no longer apply*. Second, make note of those messages that were a carry-over from your grandparents' generation; these are messages your parents received and passed on to you. Third, it is interesting to note that, even when our parents in time change their messages to us, we tend to hold onto the original messages and have difficulty believing our parents' new attitudes. See if your parents or others have changed any of their original messages on your list. Fourth, note those messages that you may have begun passing on to your own children, or to those in the generation behind you.

According to Muriel James, psychotherapist and educator, it is possible to replace many of the unhealthy messages of our inner parents and inner neighbors with healthy and appropriate ones. She calls this process *self-reparenting,* and in her book *Breaking Free* she offers ways of learning how to be a good parent and a good neighbor to yourself, based on a personal decision "to take charge of your life—turning it around if need be." In one of her exercises Muriel James asks, "If you had ideal parents, how would you be different today?" Take some reflective moments to answer her question. If you like the new self you discover as you reflect, it can be yours.

Level Four: Discriminating and Reality-Testing

At this level, we ask you to begin dealing with such questions as: How much of my energy and concern do neighbors' comments or my fear of them really deserve? To whom have I given power over me in influencing my decisions? What are my motives for doing what the neighbors want? Are some of my neighbors giving me worthwhile feedback and offering me a sense of what is truly appropriate for me?

Here, I need clearly to get in touch with critical inner neighbors and critical outer neighbors, to hear the messages each one is giving me, to discriminate between good and bad advice, and to test their comments with the reality of the situation—as near as I can come to discerning it.

One way to begin is to imagine your neighbors speaking one of your concrete fears. Psychologists tell us that half the power of a fear lies in its unknown quantity. Using your imagination, in a peaceful state of mind, allow the fear to be specifically spoken. Once it is spoken, let yourself respond to a number of important questions: If my neighbor actually said this, what would happen? What is the worst that could happen to me? To whom might my neighbor say this? Why do I feel my neighbor would say this? To what purpose? Are the words that are spoken precisely true? Am I really a snob, impolite, a bad parent, etc., or did something I did merely give that appearance? Am I really unfriendly, or is my basic shyness being misinterpreted as unfriendliness?

If, for example, you are fearful of being labeled unfriendly, reflect on your attitudes and actions specifically and realistically with questions like: What *friendly* things have I said or done today? ("I waved to my neighbor and smiled. I thanked the grocery clerk and smiled at her. I thanked the mail carrier. I smiled at the woman who held the grocery store door for me and told her how thoughtful she was. I telephoned a friend to chat.") Then, to complete the picture, ask yourself how you have been *unfriendly* today. Such concrete reflection helps clarify whether or not the feared accusation would be deserved.

When you get in touch with fear of a *specific label* that the neighbors might apply to you, inquire whether you are reacting to inner neighbors, outer neighbors, or both. If it's an outer neighbor, is it a specific neighbor or an amorphous collection of people? If it's an inner neighbor, is it a specific one, such as your mother or father, or a vague entity?

Whether you're responding to inner or outer neighbors, you can be sure *it's unrealistic to think that everyone's response to you would be identical.* When you hear yourself saying, "Everyone will think I'm unfriendly," chances are you are really thinking of one very powerful person in your life or in your childhood (whom you probably have internalized).

When you're really scared about what people might say, and you don't have ready access to your rational, logical, discriminating self—for example, if you are worried that everyone in the office would say that you were incompetent—*talk with at least one real neighbor* to find out if he or she actually shares your perspective. Don't choose a person whom you know would be most judgmental, but one who would likely be open and understanding. Whenever you have the opportunity to ask your neighbors if they're actually saying about you what you fear they are saying, do it. Ask them to give you their realistic perception of the situation.

A young woman who decided to move away from her neighborhood, partially because she felt her neighbors disapproved of her, was invited to lunch just before she moved by the chattiest of all her neighbors. The reality presented by the neighbor was that they would all miss the young woman and had always found her gracious and interesting.

On the other hand, when asked, neighbors may reflect a need for you to live up to certain healthy expectations. For example, at the same luncheon, the chatty neighbor told the young woman their only disappointment with her was that she kept to herself and did not share her enthusiasm and interesting life with the people who lived around her and who would have enjoyed her comapny.

Imagining or fearing the neighbors are talking critically about me is one thing; *knowing* what the neighbors are actually saying about me is another. For example, in the context of a supportive group (as in group therapy), you can speak your fear and acknowledge what you assume will happen to you, and you can also check out your assumptions with members of the group, letting them be a helpful gauge of reality for you. Such reality-testing both helps *specify the fear* so that it may be more effectively dealt with and helps *specify the danger* consequent upon the fear so that it, too, may be effectively dealt with.

Level Five: Getting in Touch with Your True Self

At first, the fifth level may appear to repeat the work of earlier levels, but its task is clearly different. Rather than realistically clarifying the fear and its threat (the task of Level Four), or building affirmations from within (Levels Two and Three) and from without (Level One), the task here is that of integration—the building or *rebuilding of the self.* Work at the fifth level is not only reflective and emotional, but also engages the human spirit. In the domain of spirit, I get in touch with my own intuitions, ideas, wants, choices, values, goals. In the fullest sense, to be in touch with my true self is to be in touch with my vision for life and purpose for being on the planet at this time. Vision and purpose will begin to reveal themselves as the work of self-integration is carried forward. This work can be looked at from a number of perspectives.

From a social psychological perspective, some people faced with fear of what neighbors might say are striving to break free from a life of *compliance,* that is, from living life and making choices simply for the rewards involved, or simply to avoid the threat of punishment. Others faced with this fear are struggling to get beyond the stage of *identification,* that is, living life and making choices simply to imitate the persons they admire or envy, a sort of "keeping up with the Joneses." The challenge presented by the fifth level of work is to get in touch with your own values, goals, and vision, and to fully *internalize* them so you can live life with authenticity, depth, and freedom.

From an anthropological perspective, although fear of neighbors' critical voices at first helped you to become *engaged* to your community and civilization, there was an inner urge to discover your own unique values that allowed you to *disengage* from your community, which is part of the work of Level Five. Some find, however, that the discovery of their vision and the integration of their values lead them to make a *commitment* to their community, not to preserve its status quo, but to challenge it to greater social consciousness and responsibility. That is, they feel called to become a good neighbor.

From a sociological perspective and the study of gossip, Level Five takes on a special meaning. While we realize that gossip ("informal conversation with a social purpose") has a destructive side, we also realize how powerful a tool of comparison for developing our own true self it can be. Similarly, gossip can be used by the committed person to build up the human community. For example, I realize that I no longer need to view myself helplessly as the victim of other people's conspiratorial gossip, but that I can use gossip consciously and positively as an important medium for building an Aquarian Conspiracy (a term coined by Marilyn Ferguson) aimed at making people conscious of their gifts and how they can use these gifts to nurture the conscious, loving growth of our planet.

From a psychological perspective, while earlier levels of work challenged me to uncover the influence of my inner and outer neighbors, and to realistically evaluate their suggestions at each step of the way, the task at the fifth level is to uncover and nurture my inner self.

One way of getting in touch with your true self is to *be in touch with your wants.* For example, take a few sheets of paper and begin listing the things and experiences you want. Be general or specific. Sometimes wants come slowly into awareness because some people feel that to want something, especially something important or unusual, is to be selfish or greedy. If you are tempted to stop after listing only ten or fifteen wants, take a deep breath, plunge into your deepest self, and let your wants begin flowing again. The energy behind true wanting comes not from the neighbors but from within you. Whether your wants seem to be constructive or destructive, let yourself get in touch with the energy behind them. It is a precious resource of which many people are unaware.

To exemplify the power of wanting-energy, we recall the story of a female therapist working with an autistic boy. She was at her wits' end trying to evoke an interpersonal response from him. On an intuition, she took away the toy the boy had been playing with. "It was the only thing he *wanted,*" she explained. "I took it from him, walked across the room, and said, 'If you want it, come and get it. Fight for it.' Luckily, he wanted the toy enough to relate to me, to struggle with me in order to get it. That was the breakthrough we needed to begin the therapeutic work of ego-building." The ability to express a want is a prerequisite to being self-assertive.

Another task at Level Five for some people troubled by fear of neighbors' comments, who tend to act impulsively and against their own better judgment, is to *ask questions before acting.* We suggest some of the same questions Catherine was able to use near the end of her therapy, for example: Do *I* choose to do this? Is it something I really want to do? ("Let me think about that and get back to you" was a response Catherine liked.) Questions like these help you get in touch with your own wants and values, and especially with your own sense of choosing and deciding for yourself.

Another way of acting from your own inner self is called discernment. This process, involving both your psychological and spiritual capacities, operates by means of peaceful feelings that occur in the deepest parts of you. Here's how to use discernment. When you are faced with alternatives and must make a decision, work with one alternative at a time. First, let yourself feel as though you have chosen this alternative. Try the decision on, so to speak, for a few hours, or even a few days if it's an important decision. If this alternative is right for you, you will feel a sense of inner peace deep down, no matter how frightened you may feel at your emotional surface, or no matter how effectively your rational mind argues to the contrary. Next, do the discernment for the second alternative.

When an alternative is not right for you, you will feel a lack of inner peace, a kind of inner disturbance.

We should caution that discernment—listening for the inner peace—is a learned skill. People need to practice differentiating between psychological emotions and inner movements of the spirit. For some people, intuition or instinct are other names for this inner voice. Discernment is a skill worth learning if you are at the place of internalizing your own value system and living it out in a committed way in the world.

One very quick test to take, when you are faced with an important decision and you're not sure whether you are choosing what you really want to do or are doing it simply to please or pacify your neighbors, is to ask yourself: If this were to be the last year (month, day, hour) of my life, how would I want to spend it in the light of this decision?

Dealing with this question may not quickly resolve your important decision, but it may present the issues from the perspective of your true self. It may also open deeper questions which are important to your growth.

Other Helps

In addition to the reflective suggestions offered in this chapter, the following books will provide additional support and suggest new avenues for building self-confidence and a healthy self-image. Those marked with an asterisk contain activities and exercises designed to foster self-awareness and personal growth.

Berne, Eric. *Games People Play.* New York: Grove Press, 1964.

Briggs, Dorothy Corkille. *Your Child's Self-Esteem.* New York: Dolphin, 1975.

Dowling, Colette. *The Cinderella Complex: Women's Hidden Fear of Independence.* New York: Summit Books, 1981.

Ferguson, Marilyn. *The Aquarian Conspiracy: Personal and Social Transformation in the 1980s.* Los Angeles: J. P. Tarcher, 1980.

Horney, Karen. *Our Inner Conflicts.* New York: W. W. Norton, 1945.

*Huxley, Laura Archera. *You Are not the Target.* New York: Farrar, Straus & Giroux, 1963.

*James, Muriel. *Breaking Free: Self-Reparenting for a New Life.* Reading, Mass.: Addison-Wesley, 1981.

*James, Muriel, and Jongeward, Dorothy. *Born to Win*. Reading, Mass.: Addison-Wesley, 1971.

*James, Muriel, and Savary, Louis M. *A New Self: Self-Therapy with Transactional Analysis*. Reading, Mass.: Addison-Wesley, 1977.

Lazarus, Arnold, and Fay, Allen. *I Can If I Want To*. New York: William Morrow, 1975.

Lembo, John M. *Help Yourself*. Niles, Ill.: Argus Communications, 1974.

Linn, Matthew, and Linn, Dennis. *Healing of Memories*. New York: Paulist Press, 1974.

*Maltz, Maxwell. *The Magic Power of Self-Image Psychology*. New York: Pocket Books, 1976.

Newman, James W. *Release Your Brakes!* New York: Warner Books, 1977.

Peale, Norman Vincent. *You Can If You Think You Can*. New York: Fawcett Crest Books, 1974.

Peck, M. Scott. *The Road Less Traveled: A New Psychology of Love, Traditional Values and Spiritual Growth*. New York: Simon & Schuster, 1978.

Powell, John. *Fully Human, Fully Alive*. Niles, Ill.: Argus Communications, 1976.

Powell, John. *Why Am I Afraid to Tell You Who I Am?* Niles, Ill.: Argus Communications, 1969.

Rubin, Theodore Isaac. *Compassion and Self-Hate*. New York: David McKay, 1975.

*Savary, Louis M., and Berne, Patricia H. *Prayerways: For Those Who Feel Discouraged or Distraught, Frightened or Frustrated, Angry or Anxious, Powerless or Purposeless, Overextended or Underappreciated, Burned Out or Just Plain Worn Out*. New York: Harper & Row, 1980.

Selye, Hans. *Stress without Distress*. New York: Lippincott, 1974.

CHAPTER 12

Good Neighbors

From time to time throughout the book, we've pointed out that frequently what neighbors say may be helpful and enlightening to us. Both outer neighbors and inner neighbors can be good neighbors.

Good Outer Neighbors

There is an old saying, "If you listen to gossip about yourself, you're never going to hear anything good." When Mrs. Doran was told about this saying, she smiled and said it was not true, at least not in her case.

> Twice I heard gossip about myself, and what I heard was good. Once at a big luncheon I overheard a group of women talking about me, and when one of the women said, "Mrs. Doran is just the sweetest person," the other women nodded in agreement. It was one of the nicest moments in my life. The other time happened shortly after I was married, during a party at our house. I went into the bedroom to use my own bathroom and overheard someone's voice in there. I recognized the foreign accent of a friend talking about me to another woman saying, "She's very sweet and in some ways very childlike." Her words were meant as a compliment, and I took them that way.

As we talked, Mrs. Doran realized that these statements were made by people who cared about her. Many of our neighbors aren't mean and critical, as she discovered, but people who genuinely like us. Often, even their critical words are not meant as unkind comments, but as something helpful to our growth. Such observations may be coming from someone who knows us and sees us in ways we don't know ourselves.

Mrs. Doran found the women's comments piqued her curiosity. "They provoked me to reflect on what was meant by 'sweet' and 'childlike' and how that applied to me, and how I felt about that part of me." As she talked about her reactions, she began to see how dependent she had become on her husband and how much she had put him in a protective father role. "My friend with the foreign accent," she explained, "was picking up on signs at the party and in the house. The house was clearly my husband's house, for example, and it was my husband's party, not mine. I guess to outsiders I appeared to be his sweet and dutiful child-wife." This insight, originally stimulated by neighbors' comments, allowed Mrs. Doran a nonthreatening way to recognize and begin working through some of her dependence issues and her need to be agreeable rather than develop her own values.

People experience good neighbors in many different situations. In group therapy, for example, group members are committed to help each other work through the psychological issues that brought them to therapy. Group members agree to be good neighbors to each other, yet over and over in group after group one finds that members tend to hear a suggestion that they do something differently as a putdown. Unfortunately, a piece of helpful information or constructive advice is frequently listened to defensively and treated as a criticism. Group members find it easy to recall what they considered negative comments made about them by others in the group. Yet, when asked about positive statements made about them, they usually can't remember what was said, or they discredit affirmations, placing less value on them than on negative comments. Such selective hearing often has to do with a lack of self-esteem.

It seems the amount of anxiety people have over what neighbors might say about them is in direct proportion to their insecurity, or to an early childhood lack of self-esteem. The more insecure I am, the more sensitive I am to negative expressions from my neighbors, and the threat of being rejected or abandoned. In contrast, people who are basically secure in their self-image usually have healthy self-esteem. They trust their own perceptions, motives, intuitions; they trust their own ability to take care of themselves; they trust their own decision-making process. Someone else's anger or judgment is not as fearful to the person with healthy self-esteem as to the person who is insecure.

For example, group therapy is a setting where members frequently can work out their fears of what neighbors might say, because group therapy provides real, live neighbors in a controlled situation. When, as a group member, you presume people in general are thinking such-and-such about you, you are asked, usually by the group leader, to check out your assumption with each member of the group. As you ask what each of them thinks, you often discover they have perceptions about you that are quite different from your assumptions. Group therapy is a situation designed to provide you with immediate and accurate feedback from concrete people, rather than to let you remain governed (and sometimes blocked) by neurotic fears generated by old inner neighbors.

Good Inner Neighbors

It's not solely a liability to have inner neighbors. Although inner-neighbor messages need to be evaluated very carefully, they can offer helpful information.

A young therapist, confused by some inner messages he was hearing, struggled to sort out their source. "They were present most clearly," he explained, "when I was writing up a case study to be published. As I wrote, I seemed to hear the voices of my colleagues inside me challenging me with questions like 'Can you prove that?' or 'How do you know that's true?' Yet, since I began my professional life, I can't recall a single colleague ever saying things like that to me." When the young man was asked to replay that inner-neighbor event in his imagination and to allow a face to emerge that would ask him those same challenging questions, he discovered not only the face but the voice of a supervisor from his clinical training period. "It had been his job to ask me questions like those," the young man said, relieved. "He had been helpful, training me to become a good critical thinker." From then on, whenever that inner neighbor challenged the young man with questions such as "Can you prove that?" or "How do you know that's true?" he understood the voice as intending to be a helpful one.

Frequently, the wisdom of the inner neighbor needs to be tailored to fit the needs of a particular situation. The messages of inner neighbors often come out as generalizations or absolute statements, without qualification, such as "People must always do this" or "People should never talk like that." When you discover you are mouthing generalized statements that you haven't evaluated very closely, it is likely you are giving voice not to what you truly feel or believe but to *the message of an inner neighbor.* Rather than rejecting the inner neighbor's message, examine it, question its truth and appropriateness, and see if it can be adapted to the situation that gave rise to it. Practice in editing such inner messages can often prove very helpful.

For example, parents who tend to respond to their children's unwelcome behavior with generalized or absolute judgments such as "You're a bad boy!" or "You should never behave that way!" may be simply giving voice to an unedited message of an old inner neighbor and not responding as they would really want to. Instead of either simply disregarding their inner neighbor's judgmental comment, or unreflectively voicing it, trust that the critical inner neighbor may be pointing to a trouble spot in the child's development. Question the message's truth and appropriateness, and tailor a response to the child that focuses on the dysfunctional behavior in the particular situation, rather than responding with a generalized statement that challenges the child's total identity and self-image. Messages from our inner neighbors can often offer insight when worked with reflectively and consciously.

Becoming a Good Neighbor

Becoming conscious of your fear of what the neighbors might be saying about you may bring you to a crisis point. To describe the concept of crisis, the Chinese use two characters: *wei*, which means ending or breakdown, and *chi*, which means opportunity or breakthrough. Confronting the crisis of a neighbor fear you feel may well bring you into a period of breakdown in your self-image, but it can also be a time of possible breakthrough. Mrs. Doran, for example, needed to experience a breakdown of her "sweet" self-image before she could breakthrough into a more expanded and integrated view of herself. Although much energy is consumed in dealing with the negative labels you fear being spoken by your neighbors, you can learn creatively to focus some of that energy in fostering a breakthrough into new strides in your own growth, and into changes in the way you live your life.

As we pointed out in the section of Chapter 4 entitled "Engaged, Disengaged, and Committed," in maturity there seems to be an inner drive to commit oneself to the development of community. This drive implies an inner shift in the person from being engaged and shaped by the community to engaging the community and helping shape its own consciousness. This shift in relationship to the neighbors becomes a crisis point for a person, demanding a breakdown in old patterns of relating and evoking a breakthrough into new ones. An attitude of self-actualization becomes transformed into an attitude of community-actualization, or even world-actualization. Patricia Mische, coauthor of *Toward a Human World Order*, observed, "When sought as an end in itself, self-actualization becomes elusive and degenerates into hedonism. It is in seeking an adequate response to a larger purpose in history that the human potential movement will realize its own fullest potential and meaning." Although many people do not reach the commitment stage of relating to the neighbors, this call to engage the community is heard by many.

For example, Abraham Maslow, one of the founders of the human-potential movement, and a person who had been focusing mainly upon his own growth and actualization, was motivated in 1941 "by the insanity of a senseless war" to devote the rest of his life to discovering a psychology that would foster peace in the world. In this peacemaking process, as a byproduct of his commitment and tremendous contribution to human advancement, his own life took on heightened significance and deepened meaning.

Likewise, Viktor Frankl, during his brutal years in a Nazi concentration camp, discovered that in entering life fully the key question was not "What do I expect from life? or "What do the neighbors expect from me?" but "What does life itself ask of me?" For Frankl, in his book *Man's Search for Meaning*, "true meaning of life is to be found in the world rather than within man or his own *psyche*, as though it were a closed system. . . . In other words, self-actualization cannot be attained if it is an end in itself, but only as a side effect of self-transcendence." In Frankl's words, at the maturest level of relating to the neighbors, we need "to stop asking about the meaning of life and instead to think of ourselves as those who are being questioned by life."

It seems that at the commitment level, we don't stop hearing the neighbors gossip about us and their expectations in our regard, but *we begin to sense their deeper needs and unspoken wishes for their own fulfillment.* We sense the larger problems in our world and the more fundamental issues of the human spirit, and we learn to respond to the unuttered cries of our fellow humans. In this way, we ourselves become the true neighbors—the courageous truth-tellers and compassionate workers for justice—who transcend fear of neighbors' disapproval to care for the growth and needs of others.

A mother told of a conversation she had with her college-age daughter about contemporary films.

> "I can't understand why there needs to be all this sensationalism, explicit sex, perversion, and violence," I began. "Am I old-fashioned in wanting movies to be entertaining and have happy endings?"
>
> "But I think everyone should see movies like *The Deerhunter* and *Apocalypse Now*," my daughter asserted.

> "I said I didn't want to see violence," I retorted.
> "I'm not telling people like you to see those movies just because they're violent, mom," she countered, "but so people will never forget the horror of war."
> "But don't I have a right to be entertained?" I asked.
> "I don't deny your right to entertainment, mom," she replied. "What I question is your right to remain unconscious about the horrible state the world is in right now. Become conscious and concerned for my sake, if not for your own. I *have* to deal with the ugliness that's the result of choices made by people of your generation."

Here, the daughter was truly being the good neighbor, not offering sweet palliatives to her mother, but courageously reminding her she could not afford to be naive about the precarious state of the world. She had become conscious about global violence and courageously took appropriate action in conversation with her mother. She saw her truth-telling as a responsibility both for her and her mother—on behalf of each other and the neighbors.

While we cannot all be creators of movements as Abraham Maslow was or find life's meaning in a concentration camp as Viktor Frankl did, we can be honest truth-tellers in everyday life as the daughter was. We realize that as neighbors we are here to help each other.

Appendix

THE QUESTIONNAIRE

WHAT WILL THE NEIGHBORS SAY?
Exploring Your Greatest Fears

Your age ______ Check one ☐ Male
☐ Female

PART I

DIRECTIONS: Put "1" in the box next to the label you most fear, put "2" in the box next to the label you fear second most, put "3" in the box next to the label you fear third most. Leave the rest of the boxes blank.

As a *relating person* I most fear being labeled by others as:

☐ impolite	☐ unattractive	☐ ungrateful
☐ unfriendly	☐ disliked	☐ jealous

Are there other labels in this category specially feared by you?

______________ ______________ ______________

PART II

DIRECTIONS: Same as in Part I.

As a *competent person* I most fear being labeled by others as:

☐ stupid	☐ disorganized	☐ irresponsible
☐ a failure	☐ incompetent	☐ a "bad" parent, child, friend, worker, etc.

Are there other labels in this category specially feared by you?

______________ ______________ ______________

PART III

DIRECTIONS: Same as for Parts I and II.

Regarding my *inner qualities* I most fear being labeled by others as:

☐ cruel	☐ lazy	☐ self-centered
☐ stingy	☐ immoral	☐ a phony
☐ superficial	☐ boastful	

Are there other labels in this category specially feared by you?

______________ ______________ ______________

PART IV

DIRECTIONS: Check at least one box.

What "neighbors" have the most powerful effect on you, your behavior, your choices?

☐ mother	☐ other relatives	☐ neighbors
☐ father	☐ friends	☐ other
☐ brother(s)	☐ schoolmates	☐ ____________
☐ sister(s)	☐ workmates	☐ ____________

PART V

Can you share a personal experience about a fear (in any category) of what neighbors said about you? Use the back of this paper for your response.

Thank you for your cooperation.
Inner Development Associates
Louis M. Savary, Ph.D.
Patricia H. Berne, Ph.D.

INFLUENTIAL NEIGHBORS

Table A-1

MOST INFLUENTIAL NEIGHBORS
FOR FEMALES (TOTAL SAMPLE N=231)
(In Order of Influence)
(percentages marking each category)

Rank	Neighbor Category	High School Girls (N=48)	College Females (N=87)	Young** Adult Women (N=55)	Women Over Forty (N=41)	Totals (N=231)
1	Friends	71%	76%	60%	56%	68%
2	Mother	81	72	64	29	65
3	Father	66	49	36	19	44
4	Sister(s)	27	22	22	7	20
5	Husband/ Boyfriend*	6	10	35	27	18
6	Brother(s)	21	18	11	12	16
7	Workmates	4	5	20	27	12
8	Schoolmates	27	10	5	0	11
9	Other Relatives	15	11	11	7	11
10	Other	4	2	9	10	6
11	Neighbors	4	2	7	10	5
12	My Children*	0	0	5	15	4

* Write-in category
** Young Adult: twenty-three to forty years old

Table A-2

MOST INFLUENTIAL NEIGHBORS
FOR MALES (TOTAL SAMPLE N = 198)
(In Order of Influence)
(percentages marking each category)

Rank	Neighbor Category	High School Boys (N = 46)	College Males (N = 59)	Young** Adult Men (N = 43)	Men Over Forty (N = 43)	Totals (N = 198)
1	Friends	63%	68%	52%	49%	59%
2	Mother	59	61	66	21	53
3	Father	63	56	50	12	46
4	Workmates	13	20	20	51	25
5	Schoolmates	41	20	18	5	21
6	Wife/ Girl friend*	6	5	24	23	16
7	Brother(s)	11	14	18	5	12
8	Other Relatives	11	12	14	12	12
9	Sister(s)	9	7	14	9	10
10	Neighbors	6	5	6	9	7
11	Other	4	3	12	7	7
12	My Children*	0	0	1	7	2

* Write-in category
** Young Adult: twenty-three to forty years old.

RELATING LABELS

Table A-3

MOST FEARED RELATING LABELS RANKED
FOR FEMALES AND MALES
(sums of weighted scores given)*

FEMALES

Rank	Label	High School Girls (N=48)	College Females (N=87)	Young Adult Women (N=55)	Women Over Forty (N=41)	Totals (N=231)
1	Unfriendly	30	24	28	41	123
2	Disliked	28	27	25	22	102
3	Ungrateful	10	15	22	18	65
4	Unattractive	21	14	7	3	45
5	Impolite	7	14	11	9	41
6	Jealous	4	7	7	6	24

MALES

Rank	Label	High School Boys (N=46)	College Males (N=59)	Young Adult Men (N=50)	Men Over Forty (N=43)	Totals (N=198)
1	Disliked	34	29	33	22	118
2	Unfriendly	27	30	25	29	111
3	Ungrateful	13	15	11	13	52
4	Unattractive	17	11	17	7	52
5	Impolite	7	12	11	21	51
6	Jealous	2	2	4	8	16

* A label marked "first" feared was given a weight of three, a label marked "second" a weight of two, and a label marked "third" a weight of one.

COMPETENCY LABELS

Table A-4

MOST FEARED COMPETENCY LABELS RANKED
FOR FEMALES AND MALES
(sums of weighted scores given)

FEMALES

Rank	Label	High School Girls (N=48)	College Females (N=87)	Young Adult Women (N=55)	Women Over Forty (N=41)	Totals (N=231)
1	Incompetent	11	22	33	22	88
2	Irresponsible	25	18	17	24	84
3	Stupid	19	21	17	15	72
4	A Failure	28	17	12	13	70
5	A Bad . . .*	14	16	14	17	61
6	Disorganized	4	6	6	8	24

MALES

Rank	Label	High School Boys (N=46)	College Males (N=59)	Young Adult Men (N=50)	Men Over Forty (N=43)	Totals (N=198)
1	Incompetent	22	23	26	31	102
2	Irresponsible	22	22	19	21	84
3	A Failure	25	20	21	3	79
4	Stupid	18	16	15	13	62
5	A Bad . . .*	11	9	7	11	38
6	Disorganized	2	8	12	11	33

* A Bad . . . Parent, Child, Friend, Worker, etc.

INNER QUALITY LABELS

Table A-5

MOST FEARED INNER-QUALITY LABELS RANKED
FOR FEMALES AND MALES
(sums of weighted scores given)

FEMALES

Rank	Label	High School Girls (N=48)	College Females (N=87)	Young Adult Women (N=55)	Women Over Forty (N=41)	Totals (N=231)
1	Self-centered	33	23	22	19	97
2	Phony	15	22	21	30	88
3	Cruel	23	16	14	9	62
4	Superficial	6	8	20	20	54
5	Immoral	4	10	8	6	28
6	Lazy	7	11	5	3	26
7	Boastful	5	3	5	9	22
8	Stingy	5	6	5	4	20

MALES

Rank	Label	High School Boys (N=46)	College Males (N=59)	Young Adult Men (N=50)	Men Over Forty (N=43)	Totals (N=198)
1	Phony	17	21	22	23	83
2	Self-centered	26	18	21	12	77
3	Cruel	17	15	13	12	57
4	Superficial	4	7	15	18	44
5	Lazy	9	16	10	9	44
6	Immoral	3	10	4	18	35
7	Stingy	12	7	6	4	29
8	Boastful	11	6	7	2	26

HIGH SCHOOL STUDENTS

Table A-6

COMPARISON OF LABELS FEARED
BETWEEN FEMALE AND MALE HIGH SCHOOL STUDENTS
(percentages of weighted scores given)
Note: Because percentage figures in these tables are rounded off, the totals do not always actually equal 100.

RELATING LABELS	FEMALE (N=48)	MALE (N=46)
Unfriendly	30%	27%
Disliked	28	34
Unattractive	21	17
Ungrateful	10	13
Impolite	7	7
Jealous	4	2
Total	100%	100%

COMPETENCY LABELS		
A Failure	28%	25%
Irresponsible	25	22
Stupid	19	18
A Bad . . .	14	11
Incompetent	11	22
Disorganized	4	2
Total	100%	100%

INNER-QUALITY LABELS		
Self-centered	33%	26%
Cruel	23	17
Phony	15	17
Lazy	7	9
Superficial	6	4
Boastful	5	11
Stingy	5	12
Immoral	4	3
Total	100%	100%

COLLEGE STUDENTS

Table A-7

COMPARISON OF LABELS FEARED
BETWEEN FEMALE AND MALE COLLEGE STUDENTS
(percentages of weighted scores given)

RELATING LABELS	FEMALE (N=87)	MALE (N=59)
Disliked	27%	29%
Unfriendly	24	30
Ungrateful	15	15
Unattractive	14	11
Impolite	14	12
Jealous	7	2
Total	100%	100%
COMPETENCY LABELS		
Incompetent	22%	23%
Stupid	21	16
Irresponsible	18	22
A Failure	17	20
A Bad . . .	16	9
Disorganized	6	8
Total	100%	100%
INNER-QUALITY LABELS		
Self-centered	23%	18%
Phony	22	21
Cruel	16	15
Lazy	11	16
Immoral	10	10
Superficial	8	7
Stingy	6	7
Boastful	3	6
Total	100%	100%

YOUNG ADULTS

Table A-8

COMPARISON OF LABELS FEARED BETWEEN FEMALE AND MALE YOUNG ADULTS (percentages of weighted scores given)

RELATING LABELS	FEMALE (N=55)	MALE (N=50)
Unfriendly	28%	25%
Disliked	25	33
Ungrateful	22	11
Impolite	11	11
Jealous	7	4
Unattractive	7	17
Total	100%	100%

COMPETENCY LABELS		
Incompetent	33%	26%
Stupid	17	15
Irresponsible	17	19
A Bad . . .	14	7
A Failure	12	21
Disorganized	6	12
Total	100%	100%

INNER-QUALITY LABELS		
Self-centered	22%	21%
Phony	21	22
Superficial	20	15
Cruel	14	13
Immoral	8	4
Lazy	5	10
Boastful	5	7
Stingy	5	6
Total	100%	100%

OVER FORTY YEARS OLD

Table A-9

COMPARISON OF LABELS FEARED
BETWEEN FEMALES AND MALES OVER FORTY
(percentages of weighted scores given)

RELATING LABELS	FEMALE (N=41)	MALE (N=43)
Unfriendly	41%	29%
Disliked	22	22
Ungrateful	18	13
Impolite	9	21
Jealous	6	8
Unattractive	3	7
Total	100%	100%

COMPETENCY LABELS		
Irresponsible	24%	21%
Incompetent	22	31
A Bad . . .	17	11
Stupid	15	13
A Failure	13	13
Disorganized	8	11
Total	100%	100%

INNER-QUALITY LABELS		
Phony	30%	23%
Superficial	20	18
Self-centered	19	12
Boastful	9	2
Cruel	9	12
Immoral	6	18
Stingy	4	4
Lazy	3	9
Total	100%	100%

References

Aranson, Elliot. *The Social Animal.* 3d ed. San Francisco: W. H. Freeman, 1980.
Aranson, Elliot, and Linder, Darwyn. "Gain and Loss of Esteem as Determinants of Interpersonal Attractiveness." *Journal of Experimental and Social Psychology* 1 (1965): 156–71.
Asch, Solomon. "Effects of Group Pressure upon the Modification and Distortion of Judgment," in *Groups, Leadership and Men,* ed. M. H. Guetzkow. Pittsburgh: Carnegie, 1951.
Asch, Solomon. "Studies of Independence and Conformity: A Minority of One Against a Unanimous Majority." *Psychological Monographs* 70 (1956), nos. 9 and 14.
Berlo, D. K.; Lembert, J. B.; and Mertz, R. J. "Dimensions for Evaluating the Acceptability of Message Sources." *Public Opinion Quarterly* 33 (1969–70): 563–76.
Campbell, Joseph. *The Hero With a Thousand Faces.* New York: World Pub. Co., 1956.
Erikson, Erik. *Childhood and Society.* 2d ed. New York: W. W. Norton, 1963.
Fine, Gary Alan. "Social Components of Children's Gossip." *Journal of Communication* 27 (1977): 181–85.
Frankl, Viktor. *Man's Search for Meaning.* New York: Washington Square Press, 1971.
Glasser, William. *Reality Therapy.* New York: Harper & Row, 1965.
Goleman, Daniel. "Make-or-Break Resolutions." *Psychology Today* 16 (January 1982): 19–23.
Haviland, John Beard. *Gossip, Reputation, and Knowledge in Zinacantan.* Chicago: University of Chicago Press, 1979.

Huxley, Laura Archera. *You Are Not the Target.* New York: Farrar, Straus & Giroux, 1963.

James, Muriel. *Breaking Free: Self-Reparenting for a New Life.* Reading, Mass.: Addison-Wesley, 1981.

Johnson, H. H., and Scileppi, J. A. "Effects of Ego-involvement Conditions on Attitude Change to High and Low Credibility Communicators. *Journal of Personality and Social Psychology* 13 (1969): 31–36.

Katz, Eliher, and Lazarsfeld, Paul F. *Personal Influence.* New York: Free Press, 1955.

Kelman, Herbert. "Processes of Opinion Change." *Public Opinion Quarterly* 25 (1961): 57-78.

Kennedy, John F. *Profiles in Courage.* New York: Harper & Row, 1956.

Kiesler, Charles; Zanua, Mark; and De Salvo, James. "Deviation and Conformity: Opinion Change as a Function of Commitment, Attraction, and Presence of a Deviate." *Journal of Personality and Social Psychology* 3 (1966): 458–67.

Kohut, Heinz. *The Restoration of the Self.* New York: International Universities Press, 1977.

Lacan, Jacques. *The Language of the Self.* Baltimore: Johns Hopkins Press, 1968.

Leventhal, Howard. "Findings and Theory in the Study of Fear Communications," in *Advances in Experimental and Social Psychology,* ed. L. Berkowitz. Vol. 5. New York: Academic Press, 1970, pp. 119–86.

Levin, Jack, and Kimmel, Allan J. "Gossip Columns: Media Small Talk." *Journal of Communication* 27 (1977): 169–75.

Maslow, Abraham. "Conversation with Abraham Maslow." *Psychology Today* 2 (1968).

Maslow, Abraham. *Motivation and Personality.* New York: Harper & Row, 1954.

Maynard, Joyce. *Looking Back.* New York: Avon, 1973.

Mische, Gerald and Patricia. *Toward a Human World Order.* New York: Paulist Press, 1977.

Occonner, John J. "They Sell All Kinds of Drugs on Television." *New York Times,* 10 March 1974, p. D15.

Rosnow, Ralph L., and Fine, Gary Alan. *Rumor and Gossip: The Social Psychology of Hearsay.* New York: Elsevier, 1976.

Rotter, Julian. "External Control and Internal Control." *Psychology Today,* June 1971.

Rysman, Alexander. "How the 'Gossip' Became a Woman." *Journal of Communication* 27 (1977): 176–80.

Sanford, John. *The Invisible Partners.* New York: Paulist Press, 1980.

Schachter, Stanley. "Deviation, Rejection, and Communication." *Journal of Abnormal and Social Psychology* 46 (1951): 190–207.

Sears, Robert; Maccoby, Eleanor; and Levin, Harry. *Patterns of Child Rearing.* Evanston, Ill.: Row, Peterson, 1957.

Stagner, Ross, and Solley, Charles M. *Basic Psychology: A Perceptual Homeostatic Approach.* New York: McGraw-Hill, 1970.

Strodtbeck, F. L.; James, R. M.; and Hawkins, C. "Social Status in Jury Deliberations," in *Readings in Social Psychology*, ed. Maccoby, Newcomb, and Hartley. New York: Holt, Rinehart and Winston, 1958, pp. 379–88.

Suls, Jerry M. "Gossip as Social Comparison." *Journal of Communication* 27 (1977): 164–68.

Ward, Henry P., M.D. "Shame—A Necessity for Growth in Therapy," *American Journal of Psychotherapy* 26 (April 1972): 233–43.

Yerkovich, Sally. "Gossiping as a Way of Speaking," *Journal of Communication* 27 (1977): 192–96.

Youniss, James. "The Development of Reciprocity and Morality." Paper delivered at the Annual Meeting of American Association to the Advancement of Science, Toronto, 5 January 1981.

Zimbardo, Philip. "The Psychological Power and Pathology of Imprisonment." A statement prepared for the U.S. House of Representatives Committee on the Judiciary; Subcommittee No 3: Hearings on Prison Reform, San Francisco, California, 25 October 1971, p. 3.